BANNED
IN VERMONT

4869 Main Street
P.O. Box 2200
Manchester Center, VT 05255
www.northshire.com/printondemand

Banned In Vermont

*The true story of one of the largest arrests in the history
of a small New England town –
as seen through the eyes of one of the Defendants*

Copyright © 2010 by Rosemarie Jackowski

ISBN Number:978-1-60571-100-3
Library Of Congress Number: 2011900499

Building Community, One Book at a Time
*This book was printed at the Northshire Bookstore, a family-owned,
independent bookstore in Manchester Ctr., Vermont, since 1976.
We are committed to excellence in bookselling.
The Northshire Bookstore's mission is to serve as a resource for
information, ideas, and entertainment while honoring the needs of
customers, staff, and community.*

Printed in the United States of America

Dedication

To the memory of my parents, Anthony and Catherine Jackowski. They taught me the value of hard work, without which we would not have survived.

To Dr. Theodore B. Johnson

To all those who resist war, racism, and injustice every day

With Love
to
Christine
David and Laura

*The true story of one of the largest arrests in the history
of a small New England town –
as seen through the eyes of one of the Defendants.*

Rosemarie Jackowski

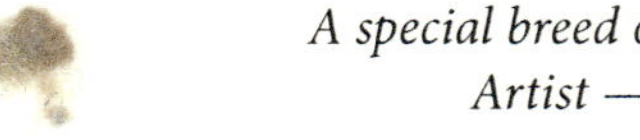

A special breed of Moose in Vermont —
Artist — Rick Havlak —

The beauty of Bennington!

Beautiful Vermont scene!

A back yard in New England!

Table of Contents

Acknowledgements i
About The Author iii
Quotations. v
Author's Notes To The Reader ix
The Invisible Candidates xvi

Part One — A Moral Conundrum. 1-42
Myths & Facts. 3
    Shock & Awe. 7
    The Arrest 10
    Prosecutors & Protestors 14
    The Sentencing. 18
    Judging the Judges 21
    The Appeal 23
    Fuzzy Machiavellian Legal Logic. 25
    Military Musical Chairs 26
    The Prosecutorial Paradox 27
    But What About Them 28
    A Moral Choice 29
    Enter The Super Heroes 30
    Questions Remain 32
    And Finally. 34
    On The Lighter Side. 36
    A Relevant Riddle 37
    Photos 38-41
    I Was Wrong 42

Part Two — Banned Articles 43-198
    A Courtroom Speech 45
    An Important Moral Question. 48
    The Texas Textbook Massacre 51
    Size Matters. 54
    Labor Pains 2010 57
    To My Dear Sister Fallujah 59
    Let Them Eat Cake. 60

Free Buzzy 63

The Death Of Personal Responsibility-From Columbine to
    Wall Street 65

Your Money, Or Your Life 69

Sicko - A Review Of The Award Winning Documentary . . 71

The Grinches Of Wall Street 73

The Backstory Of The Vermont Election 74

Clueless At Campaign Headquarters 76

2010 Campaign Statement - A Call For Justice And Ethics
    In Vermont 78

Bugliosi Is Going For The Big One 80

There's Got To Be A Better Way To Run A Country 83

Never Vote For An Incumbent 85

Monsanto's Udder Disgrace 86

Twenty-Seven Reasons To Draft Ralph Nader For
    President 89

Thinking Outside The (Christmas) Box 91

Hi-Tech Torture 94

A Death On Valentine Street 98

Coming Soon To A Protest Near You;
    A Weapon System To Make Your Blood Boil 100

9/11—Conspiracy Or Blowback? 103

A Perfect Storm In Medical Care 107

Jose Padilla—Just A Nice Kid From Brooklyn 109

Iraqi Order 81 Update :: It Is Even Worse Than
    Originally Reported :: 111

An Open Letter To Congress 115

Vermont Vets Support Ward Churchill Statement 117

God And The Red Sox 119

A Call For Open Borders - Walk Out, Speak Up,
    Never Give In 121

USA Assassination Plots 123

The Bashing Of Bennish 126

A Letter To Kate O'Beirne 129

A Thank You Note To The President 131

The New Liberation Movement 132

The Deposition 135

A Small Matter Of Justice 142

From Hiroshima To Fallujah: The Slaugher Of
    Civilians Continues 145
Here Comes The Judge, And He's Coming For Your
    House 148
They Had A Coup d'etat And We Weren't Invited
    Now It's Our Turn 149
Informing The Citizenry: Churchill And
    The Newscaster 152
Super Patriot, Ward Churchill 156
 Iraqi Order 81...Orders, Occupation, And Oppression. . . 159
A Conversation With A Hit Man -
    Welcome To Loan Shark Nation 162
Shameful Harvest: An American Tradition 167
Why Panama - Peace On Earth, Good Will Toward
    Men...American Style 170
The Far Left Takes On The Far Right: An Open Letter
    To Patrick J. Buchanan 172
A Holiday Wish List 175
No, Virginia, The Earth Is Not Flat...
    They Just Believe It Is 177
Write In Nader...W.I.N. Campaign 180
The 9/11 commission Report is A Masterpiece
    Of Obfuscation 182
Capital Punishment Because You Couldn't Pay
    The Premium 184
United States Foreign Policy Exposed 185
The Secrect That The Government Kept For 30 Years   188
To Vote, Or Not To Vote 192
Christmas On Mill Street 195

Part III — State of Vermont vs Rose Marie Jackowski —
State of Vermont vs Rose Marie Jackowski 452-4-03 Bncr
Sentencing Hearing-10-7-2004 199-251

Acknowledgements

This book could not have been written without the support of many…

Neighbors … especially the Dr. Scott and Nancy Frost family. Their on-going kindness is an example for all.

Dr. Marisa Friscia and staff… The perfect example of compassion.

Technical Consultant, Todd Pritsky. Without his expertise this book could not have been produced.

Graphic Designer, Amy Anselmo. Amy is talented, patient, and really cool.

Dale Coppin and the young heroes in the Twilight Program of Mount Anthony Union High School.

Paula Shulman-Advocate of the disenfranchised.

Those who continue to send cards, letters, and E-mails of support, even now many years after the protest…

The backstory of the writing of this book includes blood, sweat, and a trip to the ER in an ambulance. During a medical emergency, I received assistance. I gratefully acknowledge the aid of the Bennington Police Department, the 9-1-1 operator, and the Bennington Rescue Squad.

••• ━━ •••   ••• ━━ •••   ••• ━━ •••

ABOUT THE AUTHOR

Rosemarie Jackowski is an Advocacy Journalist living in Vermont.

She is a member of Veterans for Peace, Founder of Justice for Children, and has been a candidate for the office of Attorney General of the State of Vermont.

She is an advocate for the rights of immigrants, family farmers, and civilians in U.S. war zones.

As a long-time critic of U.S. Foreign Policy, the author supports the payment of reparations to those who have been victims of the U.S. - including the former inhabitants of Diego Garcia. The Chagossians were forcibly removed from their homeland so that the island could be transformed into a U.S. military base. It can be argued that the forced expulsion of the native population is evidence of genocide by the United States.

Quotations

I submit that an individual who breaks a law that conscience tells him is unjust, and then who willingly accepts the penalty of imprisonment in order to arouse the conscience of the community over its injustice, is in reality expressing the highest respect for the law.
—Rev Martin Luther King

When we talk about Justice in America we're really talking about Justice brought about by the people, not by judges who are tools of the establishment, or prosecutors who are equally tools of the establishment, or the wardens, or the police officers.
—William Kunstler

When I give food to the poor, they call me a saint. When I ask why the poor have no food, they call me a Communist.
—Bishop Dom Helder Camara

A terrorist is someone who has a bomb, but doesn't have an Air Force.
—William Blum

…the greatest purveyor of violence in the world – my own government
—Rev Martin Luther King

If voting changed anything they'd make it illegal.
—Emma Goldman

When you kill 500,000 children to impose your will on other countries, then you shouldn't be surprised when somebody responds in kind.
—Ward Churchill

Columbus did not discover America. Maybe the people who were here first discovered America.
—Rosemarie Jackowski

··· ——— ···   ··· ——— ···   ··· ——— ···

You can't claim you're for peace, if you're not willing to disturb it.
—Bill Maher

I think the importance of doing activist work is precisely because it allows you to give back, and to consider yourself not as a single individual who may have achieved whatever, but to be part of an ongoing historical movement.
—Angela Davis

You're not supposed to be so blind to patriotism that you can't face reality. Wrong is wrong, no matter who says it.
—Malcolm X

Thou shalt not kill.
—God

What I want is for civilization to stop killing my people's children. If that can be accomplished peacefully, I will be glad. If signing a petition will get those in power to stop killing Indian children, I will put my name at the top of the list. If marching in a protest will do it, I'll walk as far as you want. If holding a candle will do it, I'll hold two. If singing protest songs will do it, I'll sing whatever songs you want me to sing. If living simply will do it, I will live extremely simply. If voting will do it, I'll vote. But all of those things are allowed by those in power, and none of those things will ever stop those in power from killing Indian children. They never have, and they never will. Given that my people's children are being killed, you have no grounds to complain at whatever means I use to protect the lives of my people's children. And I will do whatever it takes…
—Ward Churchill

Civil disobedience is not our problem. Our problem is civil obedience…and millions have been killed because of this obedience.
—Howard Zinn

I believe the home of the brave cannot carpet bomb civilians from 15,000 feet and call it "humanitarianism".
—Mickey Z

      ••• ——— •••   ••• ——— •••   ••• ——— •••

*Understand that legal and illegal are political and often
arbitrary categorizations.*
—Abbie Hoffman

Injustice anywhere is a threat to justice everywhere.
—Rev Martin Luther King

*Are all men created equal? If that is to be a cherished national
value, then the color of a person's skin, his religion, and the location
of his mother at the time of his birth are all irrelevant. Prejudice
based on geography is no more acceptable than prejudice based on
race, creed, ethnicity, or economic status.*
—Rosemarie Jackowski

*If the machine of government is of such a nature that it requires
you to be the agent of injustice to another, then I say, break the law.*
—Henry David Thoreau

*If U.S. Foreign Policy results in massive death and destruction
abroad, We cannot feign innocence when some of that
destruction is returned.*
—Ward Churchill

*A patriot must always be ready to defend his country against
his government.*
—Edward Abbey

*Protest beyond the law is not a departure from democracy;
it is absolutely essential to it.*
—Howard Zinn

*The greatest threat facing America today – next to voter fraud,
the Western Pinebark Beetle, and the memory foam mattress –
is the national news media.*
—Stephen Colbert

I believe the current patterns of dissent in America are long overdue for re-evaluation and overhaul. The powers-that-be have long ago figured out how to either marginalize or co-opt dissent. Unless our tactics evolve, they will become self-parody.
—Mickey Z

By any means necessary…
—Malcolm X

—Ah, you may leave here, for four days in space, but when you return, it's the same old place, the poundin' of the drums, the pride and disgrace, you can bury your dead, but don't leave a trace, hate your next-door neighbor, but don't forget to say grace, and you tell me over and over and over and over again my friend, you don't believe we're on the eve of destruction…
—P F Sloan / Barry McGuire

Two things are infinite; the universe and human stupidity; and I'm not sure about the universe.
—Albert Einstein

     ••• ——— •••   ••• ——— •••   ••• ——— •••

Author's Notes To The Reader

Resistance to war is not a one-day event. It is a lifetime commitment – a Historical Movement that passes from one generation to the next.

This book was written to tell the true story of an anti-war protest in a small New England town. The protest led to one of the largest arrests in the history of the town.

It is my hope that what I have written will inspire and entertain the reader. If this book makes you sad - and then makes you smile at other times, I have achieved my goal.

It is also a hope that someone who reads this book will find a way to awaken a small portion of the sleeping national conscience. Where I have failed, you might succeed.

The events described in Part One occurred at a time when there was worldwide protest against U.S. military aggression.

The *"Shock and Awe"* bombing campaign came after a period of U.S. imposed sanctions that had killed many Iraqi children. Madeleine Albright, U.S. Secretary of State, made the comment that the deaths of 500,000 children were worth it. That was the official policy of the U.S. The tactical use of civilian deaths to gain advantage in warfare is a common – but illegal – strategy. The historical facts are what they are. The deaths of the 500,000 children have been officially acknowledged by the U.S.. The policy continues today – only the method of the slaughter has changed. The U.S. has added drones to its arsenal. Civilians continue to die.

The time following 9/11 was an era of heightened patriotism in the U.S. Parades and yellow ribbons were everywhere. Anyone not rallying around the flagpole was suspect.

I understand the seductive power of patriotism. I was there once. I grew up in a small coal mining town where the only

••• ––– •••   ••• ––– •••   ••• ––– •••

ix

heroes were the ones in military uniforms; where the high school teachers were well intentioned, but not well informed on U.S. history and Foreign Policy. No one ever heard of a conscientious objector there. The school day began with the reading of the Bible, the Lord's Prayer, and the Pledge to the flag. Many were so overwhelmed with patriotism that they quit school to enlist. In the 1950s, killing Koreans was a patriotic duty. Some places had a culture of McCarthyism long before Washington ever heard of the Senator from Wisconsin.

On March 20, 2003 many people were so intoxicated with patriotism that they were more than ready to accept any military action. Others took a more thoughtful view. For some in the U.S. and around the world, the knowledge that Iraqi children were being bombed was too much to bear in silence. The pain struck at the hearts and souls of many. Calling the deaths *"collateral damage"* did not change the facts or lessen the pain.

Blind Patriotism is not a virtue at a time when one's country is raining down bombs on unarmed civilians. This is a time when Informed Patriotism is required. Informed Patriotism is not a spectator sport. It requires hard work, dedication, and sometimes resistance to those in power.

Part One of the book gives a view of the legal system from the vantage point of an ordinary citizen.

I tell the story of the protest and the legal process that followed the arrests. The protest was brief – only a couple of hours. The legal process that followed took more than four years. The facts are as accurate as I could remember them, as I write this during the Summer of 2010.

It is important to note that every legal case is unique. If any factor had been different – different Judge, different lawyers, different witnesses - the final result would have been different. The fact that this case achieved a higher level of Justice than some other cases is a tribute to those involved – the Judge, the Defense

     ••• ––– •••   ••• ––– •••   ••• ––– •••

Counsel, maybe even the Prosecution, and ultimately the Vermont Supreme Court.

My Judge was scrupulously fair. My Defense Attorney was dedicated and ethical. Maybe it was Divine Intervention, or maybe just luck. It was like winning the legal lottery. I was lucky in getting both, a fair Judge and also a good Defense Attorney. Luck should not have to be a factor in getting a fair Trial, but it is.

Another reason that a level of Justice was achieved is because the influence of money was not a factor. It could have been. By comparison, the government has an almost unlimited amount of resources – most private citizens do not. Very often the side with the most money wins in Court. That's just the way it is. That is the way the system works.

I have been an advocate for reform of the legal system for a long time. Many Court cases will not achieve a fair conclusion until the influence of money is dealt with. Bribery is not the issue. Bribery is not necessary to gain influence in a Court. Money buys testimony from 'expert witnesses'. With enough money, purchased testimony can be designed to fit any goal desired. This is a legally permitted part of the process. If only one side has the financial resources necessary to buy expert testimony, and if the jury is not informed that the testimony was purchased, the result can be disastrous.

Nothing can tip the scale of Justice more effectively than money. Checkbook Justice means that many will continue to be excluded from any opportunity to gain a fair verdict in Court. Too often gaming the system and winning are all that matter. Truth and Justice are irrelevant in many CourtRooms - not only in CourtRooms, but also in the Halls of Congress.

One of the most memorable displays of Expert Witness testimony occurred during a Congressional Committee Hearing on Tobacco. The witnesses were lined up. Each raised his right hand and swore to tell the truth. Then each witness, one after another, like a perfectly choreographed ballet, testified that

... --- ...   ... --- ...   ... --- ...

smoking tobacco was not injurious to health. (Video available on C-Span archives)

Not all expert testimony should be prohibited. The Innocence Project uses expert scientific DNA evidence to free the falsely convicted on death row. Many spend years waiting for execution, and then are proven innocent and released. More than 254 falsely convicted have been set free with the use of DNA evidence. As of 2010, the total number of years served by those who were later exonerated is approximately 3,240 years. The fact that so many innocent are convicted is further evidence of dysfunction within the legal system.

Non-violent peace advocates, and other citizens, are roughed-up by the legal system every day all across the country. If peaceful protest can result in Prosecution, and if Prosecution puts one at risk in a flawed legal system – one can only wonder about the chilling effect this process has on democracy.

In the case, which is the subject of this book, there were no 'expert witnesses' to distort the facts and impede justice. I bring up the issues of money and expert testimony precisely because they were not factors in my Trial. That could give the false impression that other cases are like the one described in this book.

The Vermont protesters were Charged with Disorderly Conduct, a violation of 13 V.S.A. 1026(5) – *"with Intent to cause public inconvenience or annoyance"*. In an interesting aftermath, the Bennington Select Board rewrote the local Disorderly Conduct Ordinance. The law was changed on July 25, 2003. Was this done so that the State would not be burdened with a case like mine in the future? What will be the effect on Due Process? I am not sure how the new law would effect future arrests, but it is certain there will never be another Court case like mine. No two Trials are ever the same.

Part Two of the book is a small partial collection of articles.

     ••• ––– •••   ••• ––– •••   ••• ––– •••

Since my anti-war views became public, my articles have been rejected in Vermont. Most of the censorship is limited to Vermont print publications. More than one hundred articles have been widely accepted and published on various web sites. Some have been published in out-of-state newspapers.

A recent article about military contracts in Vermont has also been published in a Canadian magazine. It is widely available on-line, and is included in this book. It is titled *An Important Moral Question (page 48)*. One of the articles that has been used as a topic of discussion in some college classes is titled, *To Vote, or Not to Vote (page 192)*.

The banned articles are in random order. Some of the most recent first, because they address topics relevant today. The topics range from serious aspects of war, to a light-hearted children's Christmas story.

Part Three of the book contains the Court record of the Sentencing Hearing which was separate from the Trial. It is important to note that a Court Record shows only the spoken words. Body language, nuance, emotion, the passion of witnesses, the respect in my voice as I addressed the Court – none of that can be included in any Court Record. The words give only a very small glimpse into what really took place. No printed words can convey the intensity of emotion felt in the Court that day.

I did not include the Court Record of the Trial. Court Records have to be purchased and they are very expensive. I did not have the money for all that is usually required to produce a book. This has been a budget-busting project – even as I type this, my Dell PC is showing signs of failing. Yesterday the monitor displayed *the blue screen of death,* but thankfully recovered. If there is a second edition, maybe that book will be produced in a more conventional way.

This book is a way of showing my appreciation to all who were involved in the Protest and its aftermath. The names of individuals not already in the public record are not included in the text. I did not want to offend those who might not want that invasion of privacy, but their contribution to the movement is not forgotten. I apologize for any errors or omissions.

Last but not least, I hope this book will encourage and give comfort to those who continue to do the hard work of resisting war, racism, and injustice everyday. This is a tribute to all who dedicate their lives to making the world a better place for those who come after us.

   ••• ——— •••   ••• ——— •••   ••• ——— •••

BANNED
IN VERMONT

The Invisible Candidates

The title of this book represents more than my articles. It also is a way of exposing other banned speech in Vermont - and across the U.S. The banning of my articles by the Press should not be interpreted as a personal judgment against me. Nor should this book be interpreted as a failure to appreciate the beauty and other assets of Vermont.

The important issue is that the spectrum of acceptable political ideas is too narrow. Any divergence from the democrat/republican view is often not allowed. The censorship varies from location to location. Also, it is important to note that the censorship by the print Press is more rigid than that of the electronic media. I commend WNYT - the Albany, New York NBC TV channel. Prior to the 2010 election, WNYT offered Vermont State-wide candidates free air time. The offer was open to Independent and Third Party Candidates. Some Vermont radio and TV forums also included all candidates.

In Vermont it is 'legal' to use public buildings for political debates where Independent and Third Party candidates are excluded. It is legal - but it is not right. There is a history of arresting non dem/repub candidates who attempt to give their message to voters at these forums and debates. Any candidate who participates in a forum, which excludes others on the ballot, shows contempt for the voters and the democratic process.

This is not about the rights of candidates. It is about the rights of voters who should have access to as much information as possible. It is about respect for the democratic process.

     ••• ––– •••   ••• ––– •••   ••• ––– •••

Part One

> "Freedom of expression is the Matrix, the indispensable condition of nearly every other form of freedom"
>
> —*Justice Benjamin Cardozo*

A Moral Conundrum

Myths & Facts

No society can survive without legal boundaries on human conduct. Respect for the Rule of Law is absolutely vital, as is support for those who enforce the Law. But discretion, common sense, and an informed moral and global view should be part of the legal process.

On March 20, 2003, it was my profound respect of the Law that inspired my protest. At the moment of my arrest, innocent children and other civilians were being killed in violation of International Law - and Natural Law. I was protesting the illegal acts of the government of the United States.

Within minutes of my arrest the myths started. Word was out that I had single-handedly stopped all traffic through the main east-west and north-south intersection in Bennington. Not true - not even close to the truth. I don't deserve that much credit. Of all those participating in the protest, I did the least. I simply stood in silence holding a sign.

Another myth is that the protesters blocked emergency traffic headed toward the hospital. Untrue - a guard from the peace group had been stationed up the line of march so that traffic could be diverted to the side street.

A troubling myth, that still persists, is a misconception about being arrested. Not all arrests are equal. Sometimes a heroic act of altruism is misconstrued as a crime and results in arrest. During the era when slavery was legal, it was a crime to assist a runaway slave.

History is replete with frivolous, unjustified arrests. Here are just a few.

1. Rosa Parks, arrested for refusing to give up her seat on the bus to a white person.

··· −−− ···   ··· −−− ···   ··· −−− ···

2. Crystal Lee Sutton, arrested and Charged with Disorderly Conduct. Her crime - trying to unionize textile workers. Her life was immortalized in the film, *"Norma Rae"*.

3. Stephen Downs, Chief Attorney in the Albany Office of the Commission on Judicial Conduct, arrested at Crossgates Mall in Guilderland, New York. His crime - wearing a T-shirt with the words, *"Give Peace a Chance"*.

4. This is one of my favorites - the interesting case of the hungry pharmacist, Roland 'Buzzy' Roy of Derby Line, Vermont. He lived 67 years as a law-abiding, well-respected citizen. On February 6, 2010 he walked up the street, as many had done for generations. Buzzy was hungry. All he wanted was a pizza. The pizza shop was in Stanstead, Canada. Buzzy was arrested, frisked, handcuffed, and fined. He was arrested because of a provision in the Homeland Security Law. *"Operation Stone Garden"* authorizes local police to 'watch' and arrest local citizens in an attempt to keep the country safe from terrorists.

The frivolous arrest of a peaceful, non-violent citizen has never made anyone safer. In fact, misuse of the power to arrest can threaten public safety because it diverts money and attention from real threats to national security.

Another common myth is that all laws are enforced all the time. Of course, that is not true.

Prosecutors have the duty to use their own judgment in determining which cases to prosecute.

Is the Law that was enforced during the arrest of the *Bennington 12* applied equally? Would it be enforced at a time when a funeral procession is going through the intersection blocking traffic? Would it be enforced when the large group of men on Harley's come through town during the time of their rally and block traffic? Granted, these cases are different. They usually hold up traffic in only two directions. The protesters stopped traffic in all

   ••• ––– •••   ••• ––– •••   ••• ––– •••

four directions and for a longer period of time.

I do not suggest that funeral processions be prosecuted, or that the men on their Harley's be inconvenienced. That is not my point. My point is that maybe there is a better way to handle peaceful protest. Prosecutions, such as this, set up a 'them versus us' scenario and divide the community. Maybe all political views should be allowed to be heard. Maybe peaceful protest should be encouraged as an essential part of the democratic process.

Was the prosecution of the protesters an over-reaction? Could it be said that the prosecution was selective enforcement of the law based on the political views of the protesters? I would not say that, but others might. The question remains, how much real harm comes to the community as the result of a transient delay in traffic – enough harm to justify a four year legal process?

Another question that has been a topic of discussion for years – not related only to the protest – is about the selection of the large jury pool. It seems odd that some citizens are called many times for Jury Duty, and others are never called. How can that be explained? The magic of a jury is in its diversity. If it does not represent a cross section of peers, that's a problem. Given the exact same facts, would a jury composed of *Emma Goldman's* arrive at the same verdict as a jury composed of *Barry Goldwater's*? It is comforting to believe that there is some infallibility in a jury verdict, but that too is a myth.

One more myth is that protesters are motivated by the hope of some sort of personal gain or publicity. Absolutely untrue. The truth is that the loss of privacy is a very high price to pay for following one's conscience. There is comfort in anonymity.

Even Cindy Sheehan is not immune. She was accused of opposing the war in order to gain publicity for herself. I know Cindy, and I know that she is motivated only by the highest sense of honor in memory of her son. A small number of critics made false accusations against her in an attempt to silence her - an obvious ploy that caused needless hurt and pain to a grieving mother.

... ––– ...   ... ––– ...   ... ––– ...

Being the subject of ad hominem attacks is a predictable part of the process. Usually the attacks come from those in the government and occasionally from others – but they are always a part of the process.

In Bennington, if there was no fear of the loss of privacy, loss of a job, loss of friendships etc. *The Bennington Twelve* would have been *The Bennington Hundred* – maybe even *The Bennington Thousand.*

All twelve who were arrested in Bennington - and thousands who were arrested around the world in peaceful protests - were motivated by conscience. The protesters were able to place the safety of those in Iraq above their own needs. They all risked going to prison in an attempt to save the lives of others.

The spirit of Thoreau was alive and well on March 20, 2003.

Another myth is that war is not a local issue. The truth is that wars are financed by local taxpayers. Even more important, for the mothers and other loved ones of the killed soldiers, nothing is more 'local' than the issue of war. Many Vermonters have paid the ultimate price. Can anything be of more importance than the loss of a son or daughter?

Also, the myth that protesting is 'fun'. One of the most excruciatingly painful moments in my life was when I disobeyed the police officer. For me, I had to break through a life-long held taboo. Being disobedient to any authority figure was something that I had never done before – until now.

Maybe the biggest myth of all is that war will keep us safe.

     ••• ––– •••   ••• ––– •••   ••• ––– •••

Shock & Awe

The following is the true account, as I remember it, of the events that occurred in Bennington, Vermont on March 20, 2003.

It was a day of contrasts. The first day of Spring, but it was cold and felt more like winter. It was my 66th birthday, but there was no time to celebrate. The all encompassing focus that day, and many days prior, was the bombing in Iraq. The U.S. government was threatening the use of nuclear weapons. The doomsday clock was ticking. The bombing was promised to escalate into something more horrific than ever seen before. This was the day of Shock and Awe.

Anti-war protests were underway all around the world. In Bennington the peace group had plans for 'something' at the four corners. I had no idea what to expect, but that morning around 11 o'clock I put on my jacket - the red one because it had a hood. Rain was predicted. I had made several protest signs many months before and used them at the weekly peace vigils. I grabbed a sign - the one that showed a photo of a bloodied Iraqi child - and headed for the site of the protest.

When I arrived at the four corners, a crowd had already started to gather. I found a place at the back and observed all that was happening. The group was energized. There was an excitement that was usually missing in other peace vigils.

After a while the group started to march up Main Street. I took a spot at the back of the march and followed the crowd. At one point a van pulled up behind me and the angry driver shouted to get out of the way. He said that he had a sick child in the van. No child could be seen and the van was headed in the opposite direction from the hospital, but I immediately went to the sidewalk to allow the motorist to proceed. He didn't get very far. There were a hundred people in the line of march who were ahead of me.

The march eventually turned around and headed back toward the intersection. By this time the crowd had swelled to many hundreds. The street was filled and so was the sidewalk area.

··· ─── ···   ··· ─── ···   ··· ─── ···

People were shouting. Horns were blaring. Some members of the peace group were in costume. They were engaged in street theatre in the roadway.

The local police had arrived in full force - there were also backups from the Sheriff's Department and more State Troopers than I had ever seen in one place. Police dogs were fiercely standing guard ready to attack.

Meanwhile I made my way through the mass of protesters and found a vacant spot in the middle of the intersection. I quietly stood there with my head bowed holding my sign. I was deep in thought. I thought about those in another peace group who had gone to Iraq as 'human shields' – to use their own bodies to protect the lives of Iraqi citizens. Those in that peace group had reached a level of courage and morality that I could only aspire to. I felt inadequate - just standing on a street corner holding a sign.

Unbeknownst to those around me, this was a defining moment in my life. I, like many in my generation, had grown up in a culture where disobedience to any authority was forbidden. I had also been taught early on, not only that killing was forbidden, but that there was a moral mandate to oppose all killing. Now I had to confront these two conflicting belief systems - a moral conundrum - a crisis of conscience unlike any I had previously encountered.

I knew that children and other civilians were being slaughtered at that very moment. I had seen the photographs of bloodied children that had been taken previously. One photograph that will always remain in my memory is that of a dark haired little girl. Her face radiated with beauty. At first I wondered why this photo was in the pile with the others of the killed children. Then I looked closer and saw that the entire back of the little girl's head had been blown off by a bomb - only her angelic face remained. An innocent life, ended by a U.S. bomb. Would she have been the one to change the course of history? Would she have been the one to find a cure for cancer? No one will ever know what unique contribution to humanity she might have made.

     ••• ――― •••   ••• ――― •••   ••• ――― •••

War is the ultimate form of child abuse. Child abuse can never be morally justified - therefore we must either end all war, or else change the rules of engagement so that never again would any child be harmed.

The U.S. had been bombing Iraq since 1991 - a fact forgotten by too many. I had been a pacifist all my life until now. After seeing the photographs of the dead children, I changed. I came to believe that children and all other civilians must be protected by any means necessary. This protest wasn't civil disobedience. This was obedience to a higher authority.

As I stood holding my sign most of my thoughts were about the Iraqi children. I also thought about Rachel Corrie. She had been run over and killed just days before in a protest.

I could feel the heat from the engine of the 18-wheeler that was inching closer and closer to my back. I did not turn to look at it. I kept my eyes cast down and remained focused on the job that I had to do that day. I stood perfectly still and silent. I often refer to those moments as the most solemn of my life.

The Arrest

The arrests started. The crowd was cheering, mostly in support of the protesters.

Eventually there was a voice behind me. My peripheral vision told me that it was a police officer. Twice he asked me to leave the road. Twice I replied, *"I'm sorry, but I can't"*. The third time he asked me to leave the road, I replied, *"I can't, and this is why"*. With that, I turned my protest sign around so the photo of the bloodied Iraqi child could be seen by the officer. He arrested me. He was polite and professional. Though he did not say it, I sensed that he was on our side. I wished that I could assure him that I knew that he was just following orders. If any conversation had been possible, I would have suggested that he remove his badge and participate in the protest – or better yet, join with us while wearing his badge.

The Officer walked me the short distance to an awaiting police cruiser. There seemed to be some confusion there. We were surrounded by noise and chaos. I heard an unidentified voice from the other side of the cruiser say, *"Oh shit, what are we going to do with her. We just ran out of cuffs."* I assumed that there must be some kind of a rule that no one being arrested should be put in the cruiser without restraints. Several protesters had already been arrested. I patiently stood by waiting for further instructions. Eventually someone said, *"Just walk her to the station"*. The police station was only a few hundred feet from the site of the arrest. At this point, another policeman took over. His anger was apparent. He rushed me to the back door of the police station. There he grabbed my protest sign and took it from me. I asked him why he did that. He said that it was evidence. I answered, yes; it was evidence for my defense.

I was led to a cell. I refer to this as my time in solitary confinement. The tiny cell had no windows, no furniture. Only a built-in wooden bench. The bench had a large bolt attached to it. Metal handcuffs were attached to the bolt. I was now put in handcuffs.

Suddenly it was very quiet. I was alone. What a contrast to what I had just experienced in the street. I was no longer in a conflicted moral position. I had done all I could, and now as a prisoner there was nothing more I could do. The stress of the protest was fading; now there was the imprisonment.

The psychological impact of imprisonment is a phenomenon – different for each person. Nothing in life can compare to this unique experience.

I sat alone in the prison cell fantasizing about the many lives that would be saved if police all over the country joined in the protests. In a better world that is what would be happening. In a perfect world the police would be leading the protests – but this was the real world and I knew that many would be arrested on the day of Shock and Awe and many would die as a result of the bombing. I had survived the arrest and was OK - but the children in Iraq were not OK. The bombs were falling on them at that very moment.

As I looked around my cell I observed how drab it was. The walls were bare. To distract myself from my imprisonment and break the tension, I mentally decorated the cell. Ah, a picture of Malcolm X would look good on that wall. Also a photo of Churchill – Ward Churchill, not Winston. Perhaps a vase with some flowers, or a potted plant. This place definitely needed a woman's touch.

I had never seen a pair of real handcuffs close up before so I started to examine them. I slipped my hands out of them several times in order to see them better. (I am very small, so my wrists are very small.) Then I realized that since I could free myself, I could retrieve my protest sign! I slipped out of the cuffs and went to the doorway. The plan was to go to the back door where my sign was, retrieve it, and take the sign back to my cell. Just as I approached the cell door, the angry officer saw me and with a loud, booming voice, ordered me back to the wooden bench. I obeyed. I went back to the bench and slipped my hands into the shiny metal handcuffs.

••• ——— •••   ••• ——— •••   ••• ——— •••

Weeks later, a friend told me that I should not have tried to leave my cell. I could have been Charged with Attempted Escape. Escaping had never occurred to me. As an amateur criminal, I had a lot to learn.

At one point, an Officer came and stood in the doorway to my cell. We talked. We talked about our families. We talked about the war. He agreed that the war was wrong. I had a copy of one of my latest anti-war articles in the pocket of my jeans. I offered it to him. He accepted it and thanked me. He said that he would read it at home that night. In the months following the protest, I would occasionally see that Officer in Price Chopper. We would exchange smiles – each knowing that we, the kind police officer and the old protester, shared a moment in local anti-war history.

After a while other protesters were put in the same cell with me. We introduced ourselves and talked, talked, talked. Being arrested together is a very powerful bonding experience. Solid friendships were forged that day.

An officer came and told me that it was time to be *"booked"*. I smiled as the words, *"Book 'em Danno"*, flashed through my mind. I was escorted to another area and a new police officer started the booking process. He asked a lot of questions. What was my date of birth? I answered, *"March 20, 1937"*. The officer looked up from the pile of papers and smiled. He wished me a Happy Birthday. Did I have any body piercings – I answered, *"No"*. Tattoos, *"No"*. At one point he asked me if I am known by any other names or had any aliases. At first I said, *"No"*. Then I remembered that that was not quite correct. I told him that yes, I am sometimes known as *"Mom"*.

Then came the fingerprinting. Then the photographing for a mug shot.

I requested that my protest sign be given back to me. My request was refused. I asked the refusing officer to issue me a receipt for the sign. That request was also refused. After some negotiating, I was issued the receipt.

    ••• ——— •••   ••• ——— •••   ••• ——— •••

Finally, I was told that I would be hearing from the Court. I was free to leave for today. I was escorted to the front entrance of the police station and was surprised to see a group of anti-war supporters congregated on the sidewalk below. They had been patiently waiting for hours. They were gathered there and awaited the release of each of us who had been arrested. As I stood on the top step looking down at the crowd, I heard someone shouting, *"Rosemarie"*. Someone else shouted, *"Speech, speech"*. I was not really prepared for this, but still remember my exact words to the group. I said, *"Bring the troops home now. We need them here to protect us from the government"*. There was approval and cheering from the crowd.

It had been an unforgettable 66th birthday.

Prosecutors & Protesters

Many months passed. We were in legal limbo. In all, twelve protesters had been arrested. We were now *The Bennington Twelve*. Each of our acts of protest was different, but we were all charged with the same offense – a violation of 13 V.S.A. 1026(5) - Disorderly Conduct with Intent. That was ironic since those moments at the time of my arrest were the most orderly and the most honorable of my life.

The crime with which we were charged made us ineligible to be represented by a Public Defender. I asked Attorney Stephen Saltonstall to represent me. He accepted the case pro bono.

The legal wheels were in motion. I was now a Defendant in the criminal case, Vermont v Jackowski.

Our first Court ordered appearances were for the Arraignments. The other protesters chose a plea agreement. I alone insisted that we were all innocent of any crime. I made a plea of Not Guilty. I alone faced a Trial.

The legal processes seemed to be endless - Motions, Calendar Calls, the filing of documents, more Motions, the Jury Drawing, Motion of Severance, more calendar calls, and finally the Trial.

The Trial began at 9AM, on the 9th day, of the 9th month of 2004. It had some interesting twists. My protest sign had not arrived in Court. It had been locked up in an evidence locker at some unknown place. Since it was important for my defense it had to be produced. It had to be subpoenaed. After all of that, Judge Suntag did not allow the jury to see it. I was disappointed. The Defense had gained access to a video of the protest. It showed exactly what the others and I had done. The Judge did not allow the video to be shown.

The Defense and the Prosecution were sort of in agreement as to the facts of the protest. The protest had many witnesses. The

   ••• ━━━ •••   ••• ━━━ •••   ••• ━━━ •••

police testified that I had been polite. The big question that had to be addressed in the Trial was not what I did, but rather why I did it - *Intent*. That should have been clear because of the statement I made to the police officer at the moment of my arrest. For me it was all about the bombing of the children and other civilians. Nothing else mattered. What I said, and the sign I held, during the arrest was powerful evidence of my Intent. Also, I had a long history as a peace advocate, and had been protesting this war since 1991. Because of my Intent, I believed that I was not guilty as Charged.

The police officers, who were witnesses for the Prosecution, came to Court in civilian clothes instead of their uniforms. That is usually seen as a sign of respect for the Defendant. That was nice – one of the many examples of the level of courtesy that existed on both sides. Several days after the Protest, I had submitted a written statement to the Town Select Board complimenting the members of the Police Department for their professionalism during the arrests. The courtesy should not be misinterpreted as a softening on either side. There were no wimps in Court. The Defense and the Prosecution were as far apart as possible. Years later, I still struggle to understand how some honorable police officers, dedicated to upholding the rule of law, can ignore the illegal acts of the government.

The jury deliberated very briefly - perhaps only 15 minutes. The verdict - GUILTY.

There were some victories resulting from the Trial. During breaks, while the lawyers were in Chambers with the Judge, I used the time to *remind* the Press about the civilian deaths. I had access to a large collection of 8 by 10 color photographs of the slaughtered Iraqi children. I asked a friend to make copies of them for me. We had the photos in Court the day of the trial. Unfortunately, the jury was not allowed to see them. However, I did convince the CBS affiliate in Albany, NY to agree to air a few of them. They did in that evening's news broadcast. That is the only time those photographs have ever been seen on U.S. television. The CBS affiliate in Albany had sent their remote vehicle, a camera crew, and staff which included Dan DiNicola to cover the trial.

In another strange twist - the AP reported that as Prosecutor Daniel McManus was leaving the Court he stated, *"...I don't doubt that she had good intent, but there are definitely better ways to get your point across..."* The chief Prosecutor for the government believed that I *"had good intent"*. *"Intent"* was part of the legal charge that had to be proven by the State. Therefore, this case should never have been brought to Trial in the first place. Right?

About the comment, *"...better ways to get your point across..."*. I don't know about that. Remember what happened to Phil Donahue when he questioned the legitimacy of the war? He was immediately taken off air. His show was canceled. His iconic career was brought to an abrupt end. If Phil had to pay such a high price for his comment about the war, what hope could there be for an ordinary citizen? With the exception of Amy Goodman, is there anyone in the radio/TV media who challenges the war?

If there was a way to have free, open, and ongoing public discussion, there would be less need for protest. Freedom of speech is a myth. How can it be 'free' if it can end a career? Freedom of speech - maybe we will get there someday, but we have a long way to go.

About the protest sign - it was a critical part of my legal defense because it clearly showed what my 'intent' was. My main purpose was, and still is, to spread the facts of USA involvement in the affairs of other sovereign nations. U.S. foreign policy is at the root of much global turmoil. The result is Blowback. 'Blowback' is the term first used by the CIA when describing the effects of U.S. foreign policy. The CIA had been predicting 'Blowback' since the 1950s. A few examples of U.S. interference in other countries are listed below. This list was compiled by world-reknowned historian William Blum. William Blum is a former member of the U.S. State Department, author, and recipient of Project Censored's award for exemplary journalism.

     ••• — — — •••   ••• — — — •••   ••• — — — •••

** invaded Grenada in 1983
** tried to overthrow the government of Suriname in 1982-4
** overthrew the government of Fiji in 1987
** invaded Panama in 1989
** overthrew the government of Afghanistan in the 1980s-90s
** suppressed the left in El Salvador 1980-92
** overthrew the government of Nicaragua in 1990
** supported the overthrow of Aristide in Haiti in 1991
** overthrew the government of Bulgaria in 1991
** overthrew the government of Albania in 1992
** invaded Somalia in 1993
** has supported the right-wing government of Colombia for the past 20 years
** bombed Yugoslavia for 78 days in 1999
** suppressed a leftist coup in Ecuador in 2000
** invaded Afghanistan in 2001
** has tried to destabilize the Chavez government in Venezuela for the past 10 years
** overthrew the government of Haiti in 2004

The above list was not on my protest sign because there was not enough room. In addition to the photograph of the bloodied Iraqi child, the sign had a wealth of important information that the jury was not allowed to see.

A list of U.S. War Crimes, as compiled by U.S. Attorney General Ramsey Clark, was on the sign.

Also on the sign: *Killing one is murder. Killing 100,000 is Foreign Policy.*

This list of countries that have been bombed by the U.S. since World War 2 was on the sign. China 1945-46, Korea 1950-53, China 1950-53, Guatemala 1954, Indonesia 1958, Cuba 1959-60, Guatemala 1960, Congo 1964, Peru 1965, Laos 1964-73, Vietnam 1961-73, Cambodia 1969-70, Guatemala 1967-69, Grenada 1983, Libya 1986, El Salvador 1980, Panama 1989, Iraq 1991 (the bombing continues), Sudan 1998, Afghanistan 1998 (the bombing continues), and Yugoslavia 1999. (List compiled by William Blum)

The Sentencing

"Reports that say that something hasn't happened are always interesting to me, because as we know, there are known knowns: there are things we know we know. We also know that there are known unknowns; this is to say we know there are some things we do not know. But there are also unknown unknowns – the ones we don't know we don't know."

—Donald H Rumsfeld, Dept of Defense news briefing *February 12, 2002*

In the weeks following the verdict, there were many conversations with friends. Most of us did not know anything about the mystique of prison life. This was a whole new unknown – very serious business. The talk usually got around to safety issues, body cavity searches, and untimely inmate deaths. The power of the government should never be underestimated.

My appearance before Judge Suntag was coming up the next morning. I was told to be prepared to go to prison. It was suggested that I bring my toothbrush. That was a little unnerving.

During the night before the Sentencing, I was restless. In the middle of the night, while in bed with a legal pad and pen, I wrote what now is still my favorite article. It is titled, *"A Courtroom Speech" (page 45)*. I knew that I would be allowed to address the Court during the Hearing. This might be my only opportunity to speak for a long time, so I had to give it my best shot. I think I succeeded.

In some ways the Sentencing Hearing was more interesting than the Trial.

The Prosecution argued for a Sentence of Community Service. Community service is a good thing. I have done unpaid volunteer work for years. But, there was an underlying problem with the Community Service that the Prosecution wanted. I predicted that it would be designed to invalidate my original act of conscience.

     ••• ━ ━ •••   ••• ━ ━ •••   ••• ━ ━ •••

Turns out I was right. Among other things, the Prosecution argued that Community Service in a Peace Organization would not be acceptable because 'peace' does not benefit the community. I believe that that is one of the most extreme and unusual views expressed in a Court in a long time. (And they call me *"radical"*. Explain that…)

Though I always knew that I was innocent -I never tried to avoid punishment. I always accepted full responsibility for my act of conscience. Maybe a day in jail for every minute that I delayed traffic would satisfy the Prosecution. That would be fine with me. I probably had delayed traffic for about 15 minutes.

I knew that Sentencing was not a multiple-choice test in which the convicted gets to choose. I knew that I had no power. I knew that the Court had the final authority and that my fate was in the hands of the Judge, but…

My big issue was that I did not want a Sentence that would invalidate my act of conscience. I suggested that I be Sentenced to more time in jail. I had already served one day. During the Trial the police testified, that at the time of my arrest, I had been a polite protester. I also would be a polite prisoner.

The Defense Attorney argued for a Sentence of Time Served. He argued: *"…If the Court feels additional punishment is necessary, Rose Marie has asked me to ask you to impose another day or two of jail time. We don't feel that someone like her needs to be on probation, we think it's a waste of resources for the State, and she has again asked me to ask you – to tell you, Judge, that she has conscientious scruples against performing mandatory State-ordered community service because in her view, that furthers what she believes to be an unjust system and bolsters State power…"*.

I would have accepted 'life behind bars' rather than participate in a Sentence that would invalidate my act of conscience. The difference might seem trivial, but it is not. There is a big difference between being passive and being incarcerated by the State – or, on the other hand, being an active participant in doing something that is mandated by the State. Being an active participant implies an acceptance of the judgment that amends need to be made for a 'bad' act. It would have been hypocritical to pretend that I believed that the protest was wrong. And I was not about to *"bolster State power"*, especially at a time when that State was killing civilians in Iraq.

In my mind, my position was crystal clear - the State could have my body, but my conscience belonged to me.

The Prosecution continued to press for State-mandated Community Service.

The Judge said that he would not Sentence me to more time behind bars.

Seems like we were at an impasse.

During these legal arguments the Judge said something really important. He said: *"...being arrested and brought to a police station and held in a cell for a number of hours, and if that's not enough punishment for somebody who's never been through it, I don't know what is..."*. Judge Suntag actually recognized the fact that the experience of a first arrest could be difficult. This is one of the very rare times that I have ever seen a Judge acknowledge the humanity of the citizen in front of him.

About the impasse - at the end of the Sentencing process, the Court put my Sentence on hold because we made the decision to Appeal my conviction.

I will always be grateful to those who testified at my Sentencing. Their words are preserved forever in the Court Record.

   ••• ――― •••   ••• ――― •••   ••• ――― •••

Judging The Judges

"When we talk about Justice in America we're really talking about Justice brought about by the people, not Judges who are tools of the establishment, or Prosecutors who are equally tools of the establishment, or the Wardens, or the Police Officers."
—*William Kunstler*

Being a Judge is easy. Being a good Judge is not so easy. There will always be someone ready to challenge any decision made by the Court – not a good career choice for anyone not accustomed to rejection. Some Trials are enough to make any Judge wish that he had gone to Med School.

A Courtroom is much like a stage. It takes on the character of the main player - the Judge. The Judge sets the tone and the mood. I had attended the Trial of the protesters in Brattleboro, 50 miles to the east. They were arrested for refusing to leave the local recruiting center. The Judge in that case was more lenient and permissive than my Judge. In Brattleboro supporters of the Defendants came to the Court wearing *"Peace"* T-shirts. One juror even appeared to be sleeping.

The Judge in my case was different. He ran a tight ship. He was tough – very tough.

During the Trial one of my supporters was asked to leave the Court because he was wearing a T-shirt with the *Veterans for Peace* emblem - even though his T-shirt was covered by his jacket. It seemed to me that Judge Suntag, who presided over my Trial, was a little more harsh than necessary. Afterall, this wasn't a prosecution for a crime of violence. The courtroom was filled with non-violent peace activists. However, many weeks later during the Sentencing Phase, my impression of Judge Suntag changed. For one brief moment, he almost smiled. And then he said something that made me feel validated and respected. He said that he knew better than to debate with me about foreign policy.

••• ––– •••   ••• ––– •••   ••• ––– •••

Needless to say, I have enormous respect for the extra ordinary Judge in my Trial, but my view of the legal system remains unchanged. It will take more than one ethical judge to bring Justice to the masses. OK, I retract the last statement – a little too much hyperbole there. Maybe Judge Suntag is not the only ethical judge in the entire country. There are also others, but today I am not liking judges very much. The reason - right now, as I type this, reports are coming in stating that an Appellate Court has increased Lynne Stewart's Sentence from two years and four months to ten years. That is an outrageous miscarriage of justice. She is one more in a long list of U.S. political prisoners. Every lawyer in the U.S. should be in the streets and in the Courts demanding justice for their colleague. (For those who have not followed the case, Attorney Stewart was found guilty of passing on a press release at the request of her client.)

Just for the record – I know that there are many good lawyers – Lynne Stewart is one of the best.

    ••• ▬▬▬ •••   ••• ▬▬▬ •••   ••• ▬▬▬ •••

The Appeal

"Death has a tendency to encourage a depressing view of war."
—*Donald H Rumsfeld*

The Appeal before the Vermont Supreme Court went very well. Attorney Saltonstall was brilliant in court. His written and oral arguments were perfect - irrefutable. He even impressed the observers with a few *Perry Mason* moments. Some friends from Bennington took the day off from work to travel over the mountain to the court session, which was held in Brattleboro. It was a good day.

We would wait months for the Court's decision.

While we were awaiting the decision of the Supreme Court, Defense Attorney Saltonstall withdrew from the case. The reason - Prosecutor McManus joined the law firm that included my lawyer.

I will always be deeply indebted and thankful for all of the legal help, many hours of hard work, and kind words that I had received. One of the reasons for this book is to say, *"Thank you"*, to Attorney Saltonstall.

Much later, the Vermont Supreme Court rendered its decision. My conviction was overturned.

Soon after that, the government announced plans to retry me. I am still asked today how the government can retry a person for the same offense.

Though I did not openly talk about it, I was pleased with the prospect of another Trial. This would provide new opportunities to discuss the war. Also, by now the risk-benefit ratio was clearly in my favor. The risk to me personally was small - the benefit to the peace movement might be helpful. The degree of injustice in the court system is inversely proportional to the number of people watching. Many people were now watching this legal process.

I had been contacted by the producers of the Bill O'Reilly Show. I looked forward to an on-air 'discussion' with O'Reilly about the war. My appearance was canceled because of breaking news. I believe that I was replaced with a Governor. I was invited to do the Alan Colmes live call-in national radio show. That worked out very well. I fielded questions, about the war, from a broad cross-section of the country.

I was now receiving offers of legal representation from as far away as Maine and Oregon. One well-known Lawyer who came forward was Loyola Law Professor Bill Quigley. Bill Quigley is a human rights lawyer. He is Legal Director of the Center for Constitutional Rights. A second Trial would be a new opportunity to show the photographs of the bombed children.

Sadly, after the election of a new Prosecutor, the government dropped plans for another Trial – and I was so looking forward to it. Ah, the best laid plans of mice and men foiled by a new Prosecutor.

My four year long career as a Defendant was now coming to an end.

    ••• ——— •••   ••• ——— •••   ••• ——— •••

Fuzzy Machiavellian
Legal Logic

At the time of my Sentencing 13,000 Iraqi civilians had been killed. Two years later, some estimates of the dead were as high as three million.

The government defines 'collateral damage' as an unintended consequence of an intended action. Thus the slaughter of millions of Iraqi civilians was excused.

The delay of the motorists by the protesters was an unintended consequence of an intended act, and therefore collateral damage. It was prosecuted.

Imagine the iconic blindfolded figure of Justice holding the Scale of Justice – on one side of the scale, a delay in traffic – on the other side dead civilians. One side prosecuted, the other side excused.

Military Musical Chairs

One of the big news stories during the summer of 2010, was the firing of General McChrystal. He was fired because he made a statement criticizing his chain of command.

McChrystal was replaced by General Petraeus. Petraeus was replaced by General Mattis. For Mattis this was a promotion.

Here is the backstory, that was ignored by the Press. Previously Mattis had gained fame for his widely quoted comment, *"...You know, it's a hell of a hoot. It's fun to shoot some people...".*

The moral of the story is - offend the brass – get fired. Find joy in killing – get a promotion.

     ••• ––– •••   ••• ––– •••   ••• ––– •••

The Prosecutorial Paradox

How is it that a kid in Newark can be arrested for having pot; a farm worker picking lettuce in California can be arrested for not having papers; and a worker on a dairy farm in Vermont lives in constant fear of arrest – while at the same time the system ignores war crimes in Fallujah, drone attacks on civilians in Afghanistan, and torture - even of children - in Guantonamo.

The system has made a mockery of the sacred concept of Justice.

Where there is no Justice, nothing else matters. War is the ultimate injustice because it imposes capital punishment on those who have not been Tried or Convicted. Therefore, every Officer of the Court should be openly and actively opposed to war.

But What About Them

One of the things that still bothers me about this long process is the unanswered question: What is the vicarious responsibility of a citizen when his country is pursuing an illegal war? That is just one of so many unanswered questions. Maybe we need philosophers, ethicists, theologians, lawyers, historians, and some ordinary people to finally weigh in on this – actually many already have. The problem is that their voices are drowned out by the excess of trivia in our culture. Reality TV ignores the reality of the real world and seems to be more important than the bombing of civilians. How can we change that?

What about the families of the dead in Iraq? Who represents their side? Will they ever get their day in court? What about justice for them?

I am not alone in the view that individuals in the government need to be held accountable. There are many who are in agreement. Prosecutor Vincent Bugliosi has even laid out the legal case. Issues of *Standing* and *Jurisdiction* have been addressed. Judge Andrew Napolitano has authored books on the topic. This is not a matter of Right and Left. Judge Napolitano is employed by Fox News as an analyst. The problem is that too many citizens are in denial and choose to ignore the elephant and the donkey in the middle of the room. It is a matter of politics. Both Parties are war Parties. The USA doesn't have an opposing Party - yet.

    ··· ——— ···   ··· ——— ···   ··· ——— ···

A Moral Choice

Sometimes words mean what they say. No twisted, tortured, legal interpretation is necessary. Principle Four of the Nuremberg Tribunal (1950) states: *"The fact that a person acted pursuant to order of his government or a superior does not relieve him from responsibility under international law, provided a moral choice was in fact possible to him."* Principle Six states: *"The crimes set out are punishable under international law...Crimes against peace... waging a war of aggression..."* So the big question is: Was it the protesters, <u>or</u> was it those who support the war who were in violation of the law?

(This Defense has been used by soldiers who became conscientious objectors. Usually it has been unsuccessful in Court. We need Judges who have the courage to break away from the Judicial Pack and recognize the obligation of U.S. citizens under U.S. and International Law.)

Enter The Super Heroes

And just when it seemed things could not get anymore hopeless – there is breaking news – finally good news - maybe the most important news of the decade. Enter the Super Heroes – one in the form of a 39 year-old soft spoken, gentle Australian named Julian Assange. Assange is founder of WikiLeaks.

Nothing would ever be the same again. Protests such as standing on a street corner holding a sign – suddenly obsolete – like some strange ancient ritual. In the future, the job of peace advocates would be to support and protect those troops and all others who expose war crimes.

The rapid response of Veterans for Peace, IVAW, and other veteran organizations in support of PFC Bradley Manning is impressive. Manning is accused of sending the video of the July 12, 2007 war crime to WikiLeaks. VFP and other Veteran Organizations immediately took a stand in support of Manning who is in prison. Manning is also receiving support from many peace groups and individuals such as Daniel Ellsberg.

Now compliance with the Nuremberg Principles would be just a little easier.

Can one website change the course of history? It already has. WikiLeaks won't bring an end to war. Some people are not impressed with facts. But WikiLeaks has already brought an end to some of the secrecy - some of the cover-up of war crimes.

The verdict is in in the International Court of Public Opinion. The plausible deniability of the U.S. is now history. War crimes can now be televised as they occur, before the government has had time to sanitize them. The entire world can now witness War Crimes. Even those who are not connected to the Internet can see them. I saw the video of the war crime footage titled *"Collateral Murder"* on TV. That was the war crime in which civilians, including two Reuters Journalists, were purposely killed by U.S. troops on July 12, 2007.

     ••• ——— •••   ••• ——— •••   ••• ——— •••

In the end, the CIA was right. U.S. foreign policy would result in Blowback, but even the CIA could not predict that some of the most effective Blowback would come in the form of an incredibly brilliant Australian who has a passionate dislike for war crimes.

In an interview conducted by John Goetz and Marcel Rosenbach published in Der Spiegel, Assange uses colorful language. I remind those who might be offended – there are millions around the world who have been offended by the on-going slaughter of civilians.

Assange: *"… We all only live once. So we are obligated to make good use of the time that we have and to do something that is meaningful and satisfying. This is something that I find meaningful and satisfying. That is my temperament. I enjoy creating systems on a grand scale, and I enjoy helping people who are vulnerable. And I enjoy crushing bastards. So it is enjoyable work."*

As this book goes to press, the WikiLeaks story is still unfolding. Assange and Manning are in prison. Neither has been Charged with a crime. Neither has had a Trial. Neither has been Convicted. Both should be considered Innocent.

U.S. government officials, at the highest level, are pushing for SECRET Grand Jury proceedings. Will the government attack on the First Amendment be successful? Will the U.S. Constitution survive?

In one of his latest public statements Assange states: *"…History will win. The world will be elevated to a better place…"*.

Questions Remain

1. Why does the U.S. have 700 military bases in 130 countries?

2. The Bush Administration issued an Executive Order authorizing the assassination of U.S. citizens. At least one assassination of a U.S. citizen has already occurred – by a U.S. drone in Yemen. Why is that Executive Order still in place? When will it be rescinded?

3. Should the only nation, that has ever used nuclear weapons to kill civilians, have any say in determining the nuclear policy of any other nation? Should the nation that has used nuclear weapons be disarmed and prevented from ever having nuclear weapons in the future?

4. Will the U.S. ever join with law-abiding nations and sign the ban on cluster bombs?

5. Will the U.S. pay reparations to those who have been exposed to DU (depleted uranium)? Many children and others are now diagnosed with cancer because of the exposure in U.S. war zones.

6. About the U.S. genocide in Diego Garcia – it is time to pay reparations and allow the Chagossians to return to their homeland. When, if not now?

7. About the International Criminal Court – why does the U.S. not support the Rule of Law? The ICC treaty should be signed now.

8. How can the mind-numbing lack of empathy toward children who are victims of U.S. aggression be explained? During a Sixty Minutes - CBS interview with Leslie Stahl on May 12, 1996, U.S. Secretary of State Madeleine Albright said that "*...the deaths of 500,000 children was worth it...*". Was she expressing

   ••• ––– •••   ••• ––– •••   ••• ––– •••

a majority view? Is that the view of the government, or the citizens, or both?

9. When will PFC Bradley Manning be freed? If he is the source of the WikiLeaks disclosure about U.S. War Crimes, he should be awarded a medal and we should have a parade in his honor. If he is not the source, he should just be released from prison.

10. Does the ultimate responsibility for war fall upon the citizen? It is the citizen who votes for those in the Congress, and it is the Congress that finances war. Blaming the government might be therapeutic, but the ultimate responsibility falls on the voter.

And Finally

In the years following my Act of Conscience and the arrest, there was a bit of a downside. There were many good days, and a few not- so- good days. I received a couple of death threats. Though I never took the threats seriously, I did take some precautions.

In the end, the support from friends in Veterans for Peace, new friends, old school mates, mothers of killed soldiers, my family, and thousands of others will be remembered always. The others of the *Bennington 12* will be my brothers and sisters forever.

When this started on March 20, 2003, I anticipated becoming a social outcast and facing rejection. In fact, it was quite the opposite. I have never received so much love and support. Newspapers had gotten so many letters supporting me that they eventually said that they would not publish any more of them. I heard from people all around the world - some as far away as China. Canadians were especially supportive.

And now, years later, I continue to receive letters, cards, and E-mails of support from around the world - some from those who come upon old news reports and think that I am behind bars. A few folks in Europe are now praying for my release from prison. They do not know that I have not been in jail, except for the few hours on the day of the protest.

The bottom line is this - after all of the work, and after all of the passion, after all of the written articles, all of the peace vigils, and all of the protests, my efforts have not saved one human life. Discouraging as that is, I would do it all over again. My only regret is that I didn't do more, and that I didn't do it more effectively.

As I come to terms with the fact that the war continues, I am reminded, *"We do not protest to change others. We protest so that others do not change us"*. That is one of my favorite old quotes, because it forgives the failure to bring about change. Instead it focuses on keeping one's own moral code intact.

   ••• ——— •••   ••• ——— •••   ••• ——— •••

Resistance to war is not a one-day event. It is a lifetime commitment – a Historic Movement passed from one generation to the next.

One thing is certain. The Peace Movement in the future will have to use more creative tactics than those used in the past.

The bombing continues.

I now pass the torch to you.

On The Lighter Side

An Ode to Lawyers

To any lawyer this book may offend
That would never be what I really intend
This poem is written to make amends
So we can move on and maybe be friends

Some of you are really cool
You learned a lot when you were in school
You talk about things like *Stare Decisis*
Sometimes you even help a client in crisis

But do you know the most important rule
The one that is never taught in any law school
That a lawyer will never be at his very best
Until he is arrested in a big protest……….

A good lawyer will get you out of jail…
A better lawyer will get arrested with you
and help plan the next resistance
as you both sit behind bars…
                    —*R. Jackowski*

A Relevant Riddle

If the Court imposes a Sentence of zero to two days – as it did
But then the Court Suspends the Sentence – as it did
And then the Conviction is Overturned on Appeal – as it was
But the Defendant has already served one day – as I did

Does it then follow that the State owes the Defendant
a free Pass on the next Offense?

Seems that 'a zero to two days' - is worth something
And the Suspension - is worth something
And the Overturned Conviction - is worth something
And the day I already served - is worth something

Hummm, I think the State owes us a freebie
Meet me at the Four Corners at high noon…

"It's a mystery, wrapped in a riddle, inside an enigma."
—*Joe Pesci - in the film JFK*

Humor is the technicolor in an otherwise black and white world…

Standing outside the Court House with CBS, Albany Channel 6 Reporter, Dan DiNicola. Notice the expression on Dan's face as I was convincing him to air the photos of the bombed Iraqi children.

Photo taken taken during a break in the Trial. The Author is showing members of the Press a photo of a bloodied Iraqi baby. Left to right - Author, Dan DiNicola, two unidentified members of the Press, and Peter Crabtree.

The Verdict
-but I don't feel guilty...

··· ——— ···   ··· ——— ···   ··· ——— ···

Home — Where this book was written!
The monitor shows the CommonDreams web site.

I Was Wrong

During the months of the evolution of this book, I have looked back and relived the events of March 20, 2003 and the aftermath. I now come to the conclusion that I was wrong. I was wrong when I believed, as I stated previously, that the Prosecution of the Peace Activists was not politically motivated.

I now realize that my former view trivializes the influence of culture and politics. From down east Maine to the far southwestern corner of Vermont, New Englanders take great pride in their military history - *Remember the Maine, the Bennington Battle Monument, Vermont Battle Day...*

The super saturation of the culture with romanticized symbols of military battles has glamorized war. Having small children ride on military tanks during the annual Battle Day parade insures that this culture will be passed on from generation to generation.

Ironically, the peaceful protest and resulting arrests took place in exactly the same spot as the Battle Day Parade. Nearby, is The Bennington Battle Monument, the tallest structure in New England that honors a military action. Actually the Battle of Bennington did not take place in Bennington. Locals know that the battle took place in New York, but an opportunity to celebrate warfare should never be wasted.

It can be debated that the decision to arrest the peace activists was necessary in order to restore law and order. That decision was made in the heat of the moment.

The decision to prosecute the activists was made months later. I now believe that it was a calculated political decision.

     ••• ▬▬▬ •••   ••• ▬▬▬ •••   ••• ▬▬▬ •••

Part Two

Banned Articles

Topics range from serious aspects of war, to a light-hearted children's Christmas story.

A Courtroom Speech

At the Sentencing, for the first time, I was allowed to speak freely and openly to the Court. Below are my words, as I spoke them, to Judge David Suntag, in Vermont District Court, in Bennington on October 7, 2004.

Your Honor, I would like to express my gratitude to you, the Prosecutor Mr. McManus, the members of the Bennington Police Department, to my family, especially Christine, to all those who support me, and especially to Mr. Saltonstall.

It is my profound respect for the Rule of Law that brought me to the 4 corners on March 20, 2003. At the precise moment of my arrest, the federal government of the United States was bombing civilians. The bombing of civilians is a violation of international law, a violation of U.S. treaties, a crime against humanity, and a war crime. Now that same government is sitting in judgment of many who have protested the war.

Last week, in a court in Philadelphia, Lillian Willoughby, an 89-year-old deaf woman, in a wheelchair, was sentenced to prison. She had participated in a peaceful protest. Also in Philadelphia, Andrea Ferich, a 22 year old, was sentenced and she has just spent a week in solitary confinement. She also had participated in a peaceful protest. I have just been told that Michael Berg, father of Nick Berg, was arrested in a peaceful protest on Saturday, in Washington. All over this country, hundreds of those who have peacefully protested the war, are now condemned by the government. The way that this country is headed, eventually, all people of peace will be behind bars. I am in solidarity with them and all others who have resisted the government in the past, or will do so in the future.

Your Honor, it is with deep respect that I voice some concerns. How can it be that a nation, that is itself in violation of the law, can then hope to impose the rule of law on its citizens? I believe that either the rule of law applies to everyone, or else it applies to no one. Even a nation as powerful as the United States, can not have it both ways. The fact that the government of the U.S. is in violation of the law, is a fact that has been documented by many around the world. William Blum, one of the world's leading historians, and also former member of the U.S. State Dept., has authored several books on the topic...even naming one of his books about U.S. foreign policy, *Rogue State.*

I have here a copy of the Indictment of 19 charges against members of the government as compiled by former U.S. Attorney General Ramsey Clark. [*I held the documents up for all to see.*] Also, here is a statement from a group of U.S. law professors. The statement is entitled *"U.S. Lawyers Warn Bush on War Crimes."* Also, here is a report from an international human rights organization that is accredited by the United Nations. This report documents extensive U.S. war crimes in Iraq. This is just a small sample of information that is easily available. Can all of these experts be wrong? Also, I have here an Associated Press report that was released shortly *before* my arrest, stating that the U.S. was threatening to use nuclear weapons. That, too, is a war crime.

Your Honor, I believe that our government will not regain its legal and moral authority until it gives up its life of International Crime, and in the words of William Blum, is no longer a rogue state. It is important to say here, that the war in Iraq is not the first violation of human rights and International Law by the U.S. The abuse of people, people just like you and me, started back in 1492 and has been a consistent pattern ever since. Talk to some Native Americans, especially now that Columbus Day is upon us. Talk to our black brothers and sisters. Talk to the people of Diego Garcia or Panama or Hiroshima or Cuba....the list is endless.

As individual citizens, we all have rights and responsibilities. I believe that it is the responsibility of all citizens to resist any government, anywhere, anytime, when that government is slaughtering civilians. I, and many other protesters that I know, would gladly spend the rest of our lives in prison, if only the U.S. would stop bombing civilians.

     ••• ——— •••   ••• ——— •••   ••• ——— •••

I have always been opposed to any form of violence. Seeing the photographs of the bombed Iraqi children has changed my life and strengthened my commitment to working for justice for those children. I do not understand how anyone can stand by silently, while knowing that civilians are being bombed. If what I, and the many thousands of others who protested the war, did, was wrong... what then would be the right thing to do? If you saw a child being beaten up and murdered on Main Street by a gang of thugs, should you write a letter to the editor or call your congressman or write a book on how adults should interact with children? Of course not. When children are being killed, immediate, direct, and powerful intervention is called for. What the other protesters and I did should be criticized in only one area. We all did too little. To all of the people of Iraq, I would like to say, *"I am sorry. I will try to do better in the future."*

I pray for the day when factory workers join with farmers, and police officers join with poets, and judges join with veterans in protesting the illegal acts of our government. Now is a time in history when silence is the greatest of all crimes.

What happens to me here today is not important. Since the day of my arrest, more than 13,000 Iraqi civilians, many of them children, have been killed. That IS important.

An Important Moral Question

By: Rosemarie Jackowski / Published in Canada, December 2009

The U.S. Department of Offense has awarded a $1.05 billion contract to the Oshkosh Corporation of Wisconsin. Oshkosh is associated with Plasan North America, which operates a manufacturing site in Bennington, Vermont. The parent company of Plasan NA is Plasan Sasa. It is located in Israel.

The new government contract calls for the production of more than 2000 military vehicles which will be fitted with mine-resistant armor. The obvious benefit of contracts such as this one is the creation of jobs in a failing economy.

Senator Patrick Leahy was instrumental in securing the contract. The Senator has recently announced his plan for re-election. This contract will guarantee his re-election.

The chief selling point of a Mine Resistant Ambush Protected (MRAP) vehicle is that it will provide added protection for the troops. Flag wavers can celebrate. The production of this new vehicle is on the fast track and it will be used to escalate the war in Afghanistan.

The Coming of the Flatlanders

In spite of those two advantages -- the boost to the economy and the protection of military personnel, there are some issues. Is this really the best use of limited funds? The town that will benefit from this contract has a high number of homeless, a hospital in financial stress, and so many who do not have access to medical care that a clinic has been set up. Because of lack of funds, the clinic is in operation for only three hours per week and does not provide dental or vision care. The homeless shelter cannot accommodate the growing need in the community. People are often observed picking up cans and bottles along the side of the road. The 5-cent deposit might make a difference in the person's struggle for survival. Young men are often seen holding "Will work for food" signs on the roadway near Price Chopper.

There is also another often ignored issue -- the impact on the culture when a significant part of a local economy is based on military contracts. Bennington, Vermont is a beautiful old mill town. The population consists mainly of family-oriented, blue-collar workers with high values and a strong work ethic -- families who have lived in Vermont for many generations. In contrast to the "townies" are transplants from around the world. The newcomers are often referred to as "flatlanders" even if their permanent home is in Switzerland. Many relocate to Vermont to attend Bennington College. In the past, Bennington was known as the most highly-priced college in the U.S. The college no longer holds that distinction. There are also two other colleges in the town of Bennington. The contrast and unique mix in the population gives Bennington a rich culture: young, old; rich, poor ; those who have learned from books, and those who have learned from life experiences. There is an active arts community.

The Bennington Peace group has a long history of good work and resistance to war, so how can the silence about military contracts be explained? Peace activists in Bennington and small towns all across the U.S. have been silent. There is self-imposed censorship when it comes to the issue of Pentagon contracts and local jobs. The time to break that taboo has arrived.

Will the churches ever break their silence on this issue? An important moral question needs to be answered. Would it be moral to provide a bulletproof vest to someone who was intent on invading, looting, and occupying a neighbor's house? What is the moral difference between providing bulletproof vests to a gang of home invaders or supplying Mine Resistant Ambush Protected vehicles for the invasion/occupation of Afghanistan?

The best way to protect the troops would be to keep them on U.S. soil. They are needed to build housing for the homeless.

And yes, that manufacturing site in Vermont, it could be

converted into a factory that builds tractors for farmers. $1.05 billion would provide a lot of high quality tractors that could be donated to family farms.

The Texas Textbook Massacre

By: Rosemarie Jackowski / 2010

The missing part of the news report about the Texas textbook fiasco is that this is not new news. History textbooks used in most U.S. schools have been suspect for decades. Enlightened teachers have been quietly using alternative texts for years. Many use *A People's History of the United States* authored by Howard Zinn. Those enlightened teachers who sometimes put their jobs on the line are to be applauded - and protected from misinformed citizens on some School Boards.

The biased view expressed in many textbooks has been an issue as far back as the 1950s - but in the 50s too few questioned what was being taught. The U.S. never was the way it was portrayed in textbooks. Standard U.S. Social Studies textbooks are based on mythology. Propaganda sells books.

Remember those good old days in the 50s. The school day began with the reading of the Bible, the Lord's Prayer, and the Pledge to the flag. Those were the days of pretty girls in poodle skirts and cute boys with buzz cuts. The really cool ones always carried their pack of Camels rolled up in the sleeve of their sparkling white T-shirts.

Everyone was happy back then — well not exactly everyone. Lynching continued in the south but things like that were never discussed. Talk about lynching was never heard. Lynching continued through the 60s and still was not acknowledged by many.

Facts about lynching were not the only gaps in education in the old days. Most high school students were taught that the U.S. never did anything wrong. Meanwhile, the CIA was in Guatemala killing the people there. Many who went to school during the 50s were so brainwashed that by the time graduation came, they were anxious to enlist in the military. Korea needed to be defeated in order to preserve our national honor. Was it really about our national honor - most people did not know why we were killing Koreans. It just seemed to be the patriotic thing to do. Symbols of patriotism were everywhere.

Are things any better in schools now? Are students taught about covert CIA actions, about how the U.S. got its base at Diego Garcia, about the atrocities at NoGunRi? When history textbooks are evaluated, one of the first words that should be checked in the index is NoGunRi. Usually there is no mention of that U.S. war crime.

In the 40s and 50s WW2 was a big topic. Most students were taught the official version of that war. They learned those lessons well, not only in the classroom. The Saturday matinee was the big event of the week. Any kid with 12 cents got in. Kids without the 12 cents usually were smart enough to figure out alternative methods of entry. The movies were often propagandized war films. Hollywood rallied around the flag pole.

Hating the Japanese was a patriotic duty. Facts about the hundreds of thousands of innocent civilians in Nagasaki and Hiroshima who were needlessly slaughtered by the atomic bombs were usually omitted in any classroom discussion. About the fire bombing of Dresden — well that didn't matter either. After all they were Germans.

Playing cowboys and Indians was a favorite pastime. Kids were taught to hate Indians. No thought was ever given to the fact that Columbus could not have discovered a country that already had a native population. Logic would indicate that maybe the native people who were here first were the real discoverers. The European explorers, who were heroes in the textbooks, had blood on their hands. Students never learned about their criminal acts.

In the 40s kids grew up hating Indians, the Japanese, Germans, and black people. Kids now grow up hating Muslims, and an assortment of other groups.

     ••• ––– •••   ••• ––– •••   ••• ––– •••

Recently, it has been interesting watching and listening to the hate talk that has been directed toward people from other countries. If we label people *"illegal"*, it is socially acceptable to hate them. The term *"illegal alien"* is loaded with prejudice. No human being is illegal. Sometimes the law can be wrong. Remember, slavery was legal — that did not make it right. Why should the geographic location of person's mother at the time of his birth give any special privileges or penalties?

Are all men created equal? If that is to be a cherished national value then the color of a persons skin, his religion, and the location of his mother at the time of his birth are all irrelevant. Prejudice based on geography is no more acceptable than prejudice based on race, creed, ethnicity, or economic status.

The solution to the Texas textbook dilemma is easy. Just don't buy the books. This would save taxpayer money at a time when school budgets are in trouble.

There are plenty of historically accurate books that should be in classrooms. *Rogue State* and also *Killing Hope* are two superior reference books authored by William Blum. William Blum is a world-renowned historian, a former member of the U.S. State Department, and recipient of Project Censored's award for Exemplary Journalism.

Howard Zinn's *A People's History of the United States* is considered to be the gold standard of U.S. history books. No classroom is complete without it.

Size Matters

By: Rosemarie Jackowski / November 3rd, 2009

Is the U.S. too big not to fail? For everything there is an ideal size. An enlarged heart will not function as well as one of the ideal size. Giantism is a health risk. Some of the recent losses in the U.S. economy were caused by banks that were too large to be regulated efficiently. Empires don't survive. Size matters.

It might have been intended as a joke, but one of the most profound comments on this topic was made a while back by Bob and Ray Magliozzi, the car guys. On their radio program, while discussing how to solve the problems of world governance, they said that in order for any nation to function properly it must be small. In fact, they said that the only way for a government to work would be for the citizens to break up into groups of ten. Ten was the ideal number. That way everyone could be heard. Everyone's rights could be honored. Every nation would consist of ten citizens.

Think about it. How many lives have been lost because of the size of the U.S. Military. The size of the Pentagon Budget has created global harm. In addition, the size of the Black Budget is a major problem. It should be eliminated.

In a nation that is too big, there is no way that citizens can be informed on the complexities of the laws and regulations which impact their lives. Even legislators who vote on the laws are at a disadvantage when a bill is unnecessarily complicated and too lengthy. How many in Congress will have read the more than 2000 page Health Care Bill before they vote on it? A Bill that is greater than 2000 pages in length will most likely be read by Congressional staffers. They in turn will write up a brief — sort of a Cliff Notes for Congress. That's not the way our forefathers meant for things to be. If the Ten Commandments can be written on an index card, the U.S. should be able to write a health care bill in a few pages.

A perfect example of how complex regulations harm all of us was recently disclosed by Stan Brock during a C-Span interview. He made a shocking revelation. He said that free medical care would be more readily available in the U.S., if only it was not prohibited in all States except Tennessee. That was shocking — free medical care at no expense to the taxpayer or the patient. Free vision exams, free dental fillings, free medical procedures – unbelievable.

The need for medical services is of crisis proportions — sort of a Perfect Storm. Bad economy, lost jobs, home foreclosures. I started to do the research to prove that Stan Brock was wrong when he said that most States made it almost impossible for volunteer medical personnel from other States to donate their services. Tennessee was the exception.

I owe Stan an apology. He was right. I was wrong. I had believed that no where in our nation would a doctor be prohibited from rendering free medical care to a sick person. Cause of death — lack of papers of the volunteering physician — sort of a Catch 22 in medical care.

Everyone should research the rules. They are different in each State. My research is not complete but so far this is what it looks like. State Regulatory Boards cave in to the pressure of special medical interest groups. Regulations are written to eliminate competition from out-of-state doctors. A licensed doctor from New York, Massachusetts, or New Hampshire is not permitted to cross the state line and practice in the adjoining Vermont town. In Vermont, the licensing of doctors is controlled by the State Medical Board.

On the other hand, to further complicate things, in Vermont, the licensing of dentists is not controlled by the State Medical Board. The licensing of dentists is regulated by the Office of Professional Regulation, a division of the Office of Secretary of State. The rules for doctors and dentists are different. Rule 4.8 provides for a Transient Practice Permit which allows an out-of-state or Canadian dentist to practice in Vermont for ten days per year. This rule applies only to dentists.

Figuring a way to fix this is not brain surgery, but it might allow a patient to get brain surgery if it is needed. The fix is easy. Medical licensing Boards should honor reciprocity. A licensed doctor from one State should be granted the right to practice in any other State. Red tape and bureaucratic loopholes should be eliminated. Licensing fees for humanitarian volunteers should be eliminated. The lack of reciprocity across State lines denies a patient's right to choose. Worse, it sometimes denies a patient's right to survive.

For those who are not familiar with the work of Stan Brock, he is founder of RAM — Remote Area Medical. The original plan was to serve those in remote, jungle areas. Now that the U.S. has become a Third World country, RAM has held several free clinics in the U.S.. News reports have shown people lining up in the dark of night with the hope of getting necessary medical care. Many have had to be turned away.

The need for a Single Payer system is urgent. Until we have a Single Payer system there will be a need for thousands of humanitarians like Stan Brock. On the downside, reliance on volunteer services such as RAM unfairly deprives others around the world of medical care.

In the meantime, the U.S. bureaucracy needs to be downsized and simplified. Only then will heroes such as Stan Brock and the other volunteers be allowed to go about their work of saving lives.

Labor Pains 2010

By: Rosemarie Jackowski / 2010

On Labor Day we celebrate those who work — as opposed to those who inherit family wealth and those whose financial investments work so they don't have to. Many workers who deserve to be honored on this special day have come from across the border. In a global economy, workers who strive for justice in their own country must, by necessity, unite with workers around the world.

Workers from across the border, as well as native born workers, often experience hostility. They work on farms and in factories. They empty bed pans in nursing homes. They scrub toilets and make beds in the hotel industry. They work in retail outlets. They work in the construction industry as carpenters and roofers. They educate our children. They care for our elders. They have earned our respect and gratitude.

Below are typical statements made by bosses to their employees – workers who struggle for survival on the dark side of Capitalism.

1. Look, it doesn't matter if the fumes are making you sick. OSHA says everything is OK.

2. I already told you that you couldn't have the morning off. Your Father's funeral can wait till the weekend.

3. Union, did I just hear somebody say, *"Union"*? Fire that damn Commie !

4. You want a raise……..hahhhhahhhahahahhhah.

5. If you want health insurance, move to Costa Rica. This is the USA. Love it, or leave it. Besides, we don't have any sick people here. We fire them when they get sick.

6. You say you want paid maternity leave. If the corporation wanted you to have a baby we would have issued you one.

7. What's the big deal - it's just asbestos.

8. Hey kid, stop crying and pick those tomatoes faster. You can celebrate your 8th birthday tonight when you get back to your camper.

9. Next time that you want to go to the bathroom, ask for permission first. That's the rule.

10. You say that the school called and told you that your child was just injured on the playground and needs to go to the hospital. Who gave you permission to use the phone? Get back to work.

11. A little bit of ionizing radiation never hurt anybody.

12. Think of it as an adventure. Nobody dies from black lung anymore.

13. You say you want a week of paid vacation — move to France, this is America.

14. Hell no, you can't leave. Wait till your shift is over. I don't care if your labor pains are just 3 minutes apart.

To My Dear Sister Fallujah

By: Rosemarie Jackowski / 2004

My Dear Sister in Fallujah, as you hold your baby to your breast
I pray that tonight your life will be blessed
You have no water and no electricity
For bombs have carpeted your once beautiful city

How does it feel to lie in your dark bed
And listen to the bombers that fly overhead
Your anguish for your baby must be too much to bear
I want you to know that some American Mothers care

We protest and shout that there should be NO WAR
But our voices can't be heard over the Pentagon's roar
Babies aren't enemies, so why must they die
A thousand million times I've asked myself, *"Why"*

My cheeks are stained with red hot tears
But the bombs keep falling in spite of my fears
So my Dear Sister, tonight, I'm overwhelmed with shame
Because my country is playing this evil war game

Let Them Eat Cake

By: Rosemarie Jackowski / March 30th, 2010

Marie Antoinette lives. She is alive and well in Vermont. The Vermont House has voted to place a sales tax on dietary supplements and vitamins. The March 25, 2010 vote came in at 92 to 49.

Ironically, at the same time, in Washington politicians were promising 'preventive care'. Seems to be a failure to communicate?

In recent years, the medical community has finally, in a *better-late-than-never* move, recommended increased dosages of vitamin D. For decades anyone could track the higher rates of MS, breast cancer, colon cancer, osteoporosis, and other diseases in areas of the northern U.S. where there is less exposure to sunlight. There are some fascinating theories that explain the disease-resistance of the Inuit people who inhabit the far northern regions of the globe. One theory states that what they lack in sun exposure they make up with ample doses of vitamin D in their diet which consists mainly of fatty fish. The value of sun exposure and the resultant vitamin D have been well documented. Now, will vitamin D be taxed in Vermont? Should sitting in the sun also be taxed?

Vitamin D is one of the least expensive supplements. It is widely available without a prescription. High doses of vitamin D are available by prescription. Will they be taxed? On the other hand CoQ 10 is a bit more costly. It is also known to have important health benefits. Paying a tax on it could prove to be a hardship for many. CoQ 10 has been one of the leading heart meds used in Japan since 1974. It is sometimes an effective treatment for AMD, Alzheimer's, angina, some cancers, heart failure, low sperm count, Parkinson's, AIDS, tinnitus, psychiatric disorders, and many other illnesses. CoQ 10 is not a magic bullet, but it is an important supplement. It should be available tax-free for those who choose to take it.

What about fish oil capsules, and for vegans flaxseed oil capsules? Are they a supplement, or are they a food? Will they be taxed? If flaxseed oil is taxed, should there be a tax on olive oil. Will the

    ••• ——— •••   ••• ——— •••   ••• ——— •••

criteria be, tax it if it is in a capsule – but leave it untaxed if it is floating free in a bottle? Cod liver oil is available in capsule form and is also available floating free in bottle form. Here we have a conundrum.

What about red wine supplements? Will taxing Resveratrol encourage people to drink Cabernet Sauvignon instead of taking a pill? That could be fun, but will each household then be required to have a designated driver?

And what about green tea tablets? If in pill form, tax it. If in tiny bags, the tea would be tax-free. Seems a bit arbitrary.

Here's another one: turmeric. If purchased from the spice isle of the grocery store, it would be tax-free. If purchased from the supplement isle, it would be taxed.

Pre-natal vitamins, especially the B vitamins, are credited with decreasing the risk of neural tube birth defects. Should pre-natal vitamins be taxed?

For a long time the bagel tax has been controversial. Buy one bagel and it is taxed. Buy a dozen bagels and they are tax-free. Is it permissible to buy a dozen — eat one — and then return eleven to avoid the tax?

In other areas, some are calling for a tax on sugary drinks. That could gum up an already overly complicated tax code. Few people can decipher the tax regs on food now. Some food is taxed, or not taxed, depending on the temperature of the food. Tax it if it is hot – no tax if it is cold. This might have made sense in Montpelier, but it victimizes poor families who lack cooking facilities. Not every one has a working stove. If a shopper purchases hot food in a grocery store, he pays the hot-food tax. If, when he gets home, the food has cooled should the tax be refunded? Seems that that would be the fair thing to do.

In the larger scheme of things, all of this might seem trivial. There is increasing homelessness, hunger, war, and a continuing health care crisis, but some things are a matter of principle. A public policy that places a tax on vitamins cannot be morally justified — especially in a state where there is already a crisis in health care. In the southern part of Vermont many have no access to a doctor or dentist. In Bennington, Vermont there is a health care clinic. It is staffed by benevolent volunteers. The problem is that it is open only three hours per week and it does not offer dental or vision care. Dental care would go a long way in assuring health. It should be at the top of the list for preventive care. There is not much recognition of that fact in Washington or in Montpelier. Eventually the Legislature reversed its position and the Vitamin Tax was not adopted.

The federal tax code is not any better than most state codes. Some needed improvements are obvious. Simplify the code. Eliminate most deductions. Make it fair. A progressive tax that starts at 1 % on incomes above $88,000 would be an improvement. The tax could progressively increase to 100% on incomes above $1,000,000. Most important: eliminate the cap on the Social Security tax and include all income, earned and unearned. Make it a progressive tax that is fair to low wage workers.

The worse thing about a tax on vitamins might not be the adverse health effect that will result. The worse thing is that this is a regressive tax – hurting those who can least afford it. Instead of taxing vitamins, vitamins should be given free to all who could benefit from them. This could be paid for by placing a progressive tax on all incomes — earned and unearned — above a certain amount. Maybe $88,000 would be a good place to start the discussion. Seems that that would be the neighborly thing to do. Pay for your neighbor's vitamins if your income is above $88,000.

     ••• ——— •••   ••• ——— •••   ••• ——— •••

Free Buzzy

By: Rosemarie Jackowski / March 17th, 2010

It was just a matter of time. This was sure to happen. All he really wanted was a pizza. He wanted a pizza pie so much that he walked to another country to get one. Well, he really did not walk very far. The pizza shop was just up the street a short distance from his own business, the town pharmacy. He and many others have been walking up and down this street without incident for generations.

Stanstead and Derby Line just happen to be in two different countries. Stanstead is in Canada and Derby Line is in the U.S. That was never a problem — that is until Homeland Security arrived on the scene with Operation Stone Garden — a little known federal plan which uses local police to 'watch' citizens. Is that really a good idea?

I admit that the guys in uniforms with the guns are faced with a bit of a conundrum — what to do when the international border is in the middle of a close-knit rural community. The local library is straddling the international border. The locals get the books from the shelves in one country and check them out in the same building at the desk which happens to be on the other side of the international border. The pizza shop is in Stanstead, Quebec. The hungry pharmacist was in Derby Line, Vermont.

Used to be that when Aunt Millie in Stanstead needed to borrow a cup of sugar she just walked down to her niece's house in Derby Line. But then came the restrictions — border guards, gates blocking the village streets. The quiet, little village was now under siege.

It has been reported that snow plow drivers were among the first to have problems. They could no longer turn their plows around. They were finally issued keys to unlock the gates so that they could drive through the barricades.

Now we have the interesting case of the hungry pharmacist,

Roland 'Buzz' Roy. He lived 67 years as a law abiding citizen, but then on February 6, 2010 he walked across the border to the pizza shop. Yep, you guessed it. He was frisked, handcuffed, and fined. Early reports said that he was fined $5000. That amount has now been reduced to $500. That's a lot to pay for a pizza — even a pizza with 'the works', loaded with all of the good stuff.

Local residents stand firmly in support of 'Buzzy' and a protest in his honor is planned for March 27. The 'Free Buzzy' movement is in full swing.

On March 20, 2003 there was a large protest of the war at the other end of the State of Vermont. One of the largest arrests in town history was made that day. The Bennington 12 were arrested for their peaceful protest of 'Shock and Awe'. That was a day to remember. Shortly after the arrests, the town officers had second thoughts about the law in question. They, in their infinite wisdom, rewrote the law so that peaceful protesters in the future would not be exposed to the same complex legal process. In the end, the government officials decided that there was a better way to use tax-payer funds.

In Derby Line hopefully someone will step up to the plate so that common sense will prevail. In the meantime — Free 'Buzzy', and free pizza for everybody. And watch out for that guy hiding behind the tree. He just might be part of Operation Stone Garden.

     ••• – – – •••   ••• – – – •••   ••• – – – •••

The Death Of Personal Responsibility - From Columbine to Wall Street

By: Rosemarie Jackowski / October 19th, 2009

Susan Klebold, mother of Dylan Klebold, one of the Columbine Shooters, has released an essay that is now widely publicized. It was originally published in O Magazine. In her article, Susan says, *"For the rest of my life, I will be haunted by the horror and anguish Dylan caused. I cannot look at a child in a grocery store or on the street without thinking about how my son's schoolmates spent the last moments of their lives. Dylan changed everything I believed about myself, about God, about family and about love."*

Blogs that responded to the essay contain some interesting comments. Many bloggers blame poor parenting for the shootings. Many others describe a deep sense of compassion for Susan and show a greater level of understanding of the human condition.

Life can be complicated. Dave Pelzer is author of *A Child Called It*. He has never demonstrated any anti-social behavior. It appears that as a child, he was the victim of extreme abuse.

On the other hand, it appears that Ted Kaczynski, the Unabomber, had a normal, loving childhood. His brother, David, is a highly respected member of the community. They grew up in the same home. The causes of criminal/ anti-social behavior are complex and not completely understood.

There can be no greater pain than the death of a child, except maybe having a son who kills others and then himself. Susan Klebold is now a member of a very exclusive club of parents and other family members who have suffered that extreme horror. The family of the Virginia Tech Shooter, the mother and brother of the Unabomber, and many others have a loved one who has murdered. They are too often held responsible for the crimes of their loved ones. How much responsibility do these family members have for

••• ――― •••   ••• ――― •••   ••• ――― •••

the actions of the offender? None – they are not to blame. They, too, are innocent victims. Often they had no way of predicting the criminal act. Sometimes, even if the family had recognized warning signs, they still could not have prevented the horrific act. HIPA and other limits in our health care system act as roadblocks to mental health care. The Virginia Tech shooter had a history of counseling for mental health problems. Parents often are not given access to the student's academic records, let alone health records.

We have morphed into a culture of *blame-the-other-guy. I didn't mean to do it. It was a mistake. The dog ate my homework. My wife doesn't understand me. My husband doesn't pay enough attention to me. Buyer beware. My mother didn't love me enough. My father didn't talk to me enough. It was just a campaign promise. The media lied to me. Everybody else is doing it. The bad economy made me enlist. I was just following orders.*

Wall Street Bankers hoard a large portion of the national wealth and blame it on their compensation boards. Congress has written the legislation that allows such greed. The members of Congress blame the lobbyists. The lobbyists say they are just doing their job. The voters say that they have been misled by the media. The media says that they have to put ratings first. We are witnessing the death of personal responsibility.

Capitalism is a big contributor to the problem; but, voters do not have to vote for capitalists. On my ballot there were eight candidates for president, plus a write-in option. Voting has consequences. Uninformed voting has disastrous consequences. Voters say blame someone else. They say that they do not have time to research the issues. An uninformed voter is dangerous and should stay home on election day. It is better to not vote at all, than to cast an uninformed ballot and cancel the vote of someone who has studied the issues.

The lack of compassion is blocking real health care reform. We need Reform School for the compassionless. The *every-man-for-himself* culture was especially evident during the health care town meetings. It was common to hear comments such as, *"I am insured – the hell with everybody else". Raise-the-drawbridge syndrome —* I am safe and you don't count.

A pervasive lack of personal responsibility exists in local and national governments – also as a business model in the corporate world. Decisions are often made by committee in order to distance one from any singular responsibility. Temporary Experts are often hired for the sole purpose of relieving others from the consequences of a decision. Passing the buck has become a national pastime. It's enough to make one wish for the end of the government system as we know it — to be replaced by a Benevolent Monarchy. No more hiding behind Experts and committee group decisions.

The culture of the Internet is not helping. Bloggers usually prefer anonymity when dropping comments. Why the failure to accept responsibility for the comment left on the blog? The civility of the blogosphere would be greatly improved if everyone gave an honest identification.

The brain is an organ – in some ways like a pancreas or a liver. It is affected by genetics, age, drugs, the environment, electrical currents, illness, and an unknown number of other influences. Where should the line between evil and madness be drawn? And who should make that determination?

Psychiatrists will continue to debate the ability of a patient to make ethical judgments. Philosophers will continue to debate Free Will versus Determinism. Lawyers will continue to argue for the guilt or innocence of the accused; but, the simple fact is that a society which is organized on any principle that does not include personal responsibility will not work.

The bottom line is that everyone must be held responsible for their own actions, and no one should ever be held responsible for the acts of another. What a revolutionary concept.

News reports are filled with senseless acts of violence. Today's report is about a group of teens who set a 15 year old boy on fire and then laughed as they watched him burn. We must do better. We must find a way to develop empathy and compassion. The teens who set the fire must be held accountable for their act. You and I, as members of society, must be held responsible for the culture of violence that disables the youthful conscience.

Susan Klebold should be held responsible, and maybe praised, for her parenting. She should never be held responsible for the acts of Dylan.

Your Money, Or Your Life

By: Rosemarie Jackowski / September 28th, 2009

Death is not optional. It will come to all of us sooner or later. The best that can be hoped for is to have a life that is long and a death that is as painless as possible.

Forty-three year old Edith Rodriguez lost on both of those counts. Her life was needlessly brought to a tragic end. She spent her last time on earth writhing in pain. Why? Was Edith in some desolate third world country? No, she was in the United States. Was Edith in an isolated location, far from medical help? No, she was in the Emergency Room of a California hospital. Was this tragedy caused by the fact that she might not have had health insurance? Maybe. Was the problem that she was sick while being Hispanic? Could be.

The news reports have painted a picture that is difficult to think about. Edith writhing in pain in the Emergency Room — falling out of the wheel chair, vomiting blood while lying on the cold Emergency Room floor, excruciating pain, a possible bowel perforation — the janitorial staff cleaning the floor around her limp body, while the medical staff ignored the pleas for help from her family. This is not meant to be a condemnation of all doctors, nurses, and other medical personnel. It is meant to be a condemnation of the system, a system that has lost any hint of humanity.

Why did no one help Edith? What mistake did Edith make that caused this tragedy? Was this death-by-geography? If Edith had been almost anywhere else in the industrialized world, she probably would still be alive. She died because she was in the United States. Living in the U.S. can be hazardous to your health. This is a nation that puts profits before patients; capitalism before compassion.

Sadly, Edith is not alone. In the United States 45,000 die every year from lack of medical care. That is like having fifteen 9/11s every year. It is worse than 9/11 because these are needless deaths that we are imposing on ourselves. These deaths will continue until there is a strong grassroots movement for a universal, single payer health care system.

Think that the Democrats or the Republicans will change things? Think again. Both political parties have been bought and paid for by the lobbyists. It is the lobbyists for the pharmaceutical companies, the HMOs, the insurance companies, and the for-profit medical centers who lurk through the halls of Congress and help write the legislation.

The U.S. is in a crisis. Extortion by Insurance Company lobbyists must end. We need a Single Payer system immediately. Single Payer will save lives, and it also will save money. The exorbitant salaries of Insurance Company CEOs will be eliminated. The profit motive for investors will be eliminated. Administrative costs will be reduced because one single payer will replace a large number of insurance companies — all with different forms, different standards, and different requirements for an endless stream of confusing paper work. Single Payer will save money. Repeating, Single Payer will save money.

Health care by Wall Street standards does not work. Just ask the family of Edith Rodriguez.

Sicko - A Review Of The Award Winning Documentary

By: Rosemarie Jackowski / July 2007

An Open Letter to Michael Moore

Hey there Mike...

I just left the theater where I saw SiCKO. While I am still all charged up on the evils of Capitalism, I thought that I'd dash this note off to you. On a scale of 1 to 10, with 10 being as good as it gets, I rate SiCKO a perfect 10. I would have given a score of 12 - a score reserved for the best film ever produced - except for about 45 seconds of SiCKO that should have been left on the cutting room floor. You made two mistakes. When you went to Gitmo, you said that you were on U.S. property. I can show you a few thousand Cubans who might challenge that statement. Your second mistake was a more serious one. You implied that the Gitmo prisoners are well cared for. You ignored the fact that, although they might receive good medical care, they are also tortured. How many suicides have there been among the Gitmo prisoners?

OK, now that the negative part of the movie review is done, I can say that SiCKO is a masterpiece. You succeeded in exactly the right balance of emotional appeal, fact giving, and humor. Anyone, who does not see this movie, is missing a treat and an education. It is a film that should be included in every high school curriculum. One of the important points made in the film is the comparison between the U.S. and other countries. The locations selected for the filming were perfect. I almost felt like I was in the apartment in France. The differences in culture and attitude were apparent. In the U.S. we have an "every man for himself" type philosophy. In other countries, there is compassion for fellow citizens.

While watching the movie, I was impressed with the teeth of those in the film. That may seem like a minor detail - but not if you live where I do. Many take dental health for granted, but in some areas of the United States dental care is considered a luxury. One of my friends actually relocated to Costa Rica because she needed a dentist.

You made the often-overlooked point that in the USA, 45,000 die every year from lack of access to medical care. That is like having a 9/11 every 30 days, but worse. We are imposing those 45,000 deaths on ourselves. You also made the point that the quality of care in the U.S. is often deficient, as when the sick and elderly patients in California were thrown out of taxicabs on the pavement.

The most important point of the film might be the explanation about the cause of the problem in the United States. You very clearly show the deadly effect of the greed of politicians and insurance companies. I was left wondering who are the real terrorists. Insurance Company "denials-of-care" kill more people than foreign enemies invading our shores do. Though the film does not exactly come out and say it, the solution is obvious. We have to get Wall Street out of the health care industry. A single-payer system would save lives and money.

Your film might cause an exodus from the United States. You say that in Canada it helps to be married to a Canadian. I wonder if I can make it to the border before dark and if I can *"hook-a-Canuck"* there. I do windows and make a great pot of chicken soup. Thanks for this one, Mike. I can't wait for your next project.

     ••• ——— •••   ••• ——— •••   ••• ——— •••

The Grinches Of Wall Street

By: Rosemarie Jackowski / December 8th, 2008

'Twas the night before Christmas
And through the Senate and House
The money was flowing
To each Wall Street louse

The hedge fund managers and CEOs
Had told their tales of financial woes
Their stories were naughty – not very nice
They told of private jets and gluttonous vice

Meanwhile on Main Street the people were sad
No one could explain why things had gotten so bad
Some said the cause was market speculation
Others said Capitalism was the right explanation

Santa's elves should create a People's State
End all war, poverty, and hate
A Single Payer System would keep us healthy
Enough food for all – no need to be wealthy

At the shelter, the children were snuggled in their beds
As nightmares of foreclosure danced through their heads
A holiday miracle is what we need
On second thought – we just might have to secede

The Backstory Of The Vermont Election

By: Rosemarie Jackowski / November 29th, 2008

One of the important things that happened during this recent campaign season was the censoring by the Press of non democratic/republican candidates. This has been a nation-wide problem for a long time. The 'Naderization' of candidates is a growing threat to the electoral process.

Nowhere in the country has the problem with the Press been more serious than in the southern half of Vermont. Letters of support of non major Party candidates were not published. Campaign statements were not published. There was total news blackout in most of southern Vermont. Voters had almost no access to relevant candidate information.

This news blackout was so extreme that newspapers in the southern part of Vermont even refused to insert the Candidate Information Publication. This official, non-partisan publication had been authorized by the Vermont Legislature (17 V.S.A. 2810 b) and paid for by the taxpayers. As a contrast, newspapers in the central and northern parts of Vermont such as The Burlington Free Press, The Newport Daily News, The Rutland Herald, and The Times Argus inserted and distributed the publication. Those newspapers are to be commended for their public service.

The Office of Secretary of State is to be commended for sending more than a thousand copies of the publication to a private citizen in the southern part of the State. As a last resort, the citizen had volunteered to distribute the publication – a much less efficient system of distribution than insertion in the daily newspaper.

It is now necessary for the legislature to rewrite the law so that southern Vermont will have access to relevant information. Two amendments to the law (17 V.S.A. 2810b) are recommended. First, set a publication date for the Candidate Information Publication

 ••• ——— •••   ••• ——— •••   ••• ——— •••

that would precede the first day allowed for absentee voting. Becoming an informed voter after casting the ballot is not the proper sequence of events. Second, the law must provide for a plan of distribution in the southern part of the State.

In Vermont, and across the country, many have no access to the Internet. Some areas are not in a major media market; therefore, TV news is non existent. The newspaper is the only source of information – the lifeline of the community. It is that which transforms individuals into a community. In rural USA there is no voice that is more powerful than that of the local newspaper. When any newspaper fails in its sacred mission, the community is harmed.

The Vermont news blackout has had serious consequences. Not only were ordinary voters uninformed, but even campaign workers – usually a well-informed group of activists – were so lacking in information that it inspired an article, 'Clueless at Campaign Headquarters'. The article describes a phone call received from campaign headquarters in southern Vermont. The worker was not aware that there were any candidates on the ballot other than McCain and Obama. In Vermont there were eight candidates for president on the ballot. Many Vermonters were unprepared to see so many names on the ballot when they entered the voting booth.

Private companies that own newspapers have editorial rights. That right should be respected. Every newspaper has the right to print, or not print, anything it wants. That is not the issue. The issue is the lack of journalistic ethics. Ethics are not required by law – or are they? If any individual interfered with the electoral process in such an extreme way that it influenced the outcome of an election, would it be acceptable?

What occurred in Vermont was an extreme violation that resulted in many ripple effects on the outcome of the election. One such effect was that the Liberty Union/Socialist Party lost Major Party Status and all of the legal rights that accompany that status.

There can be no democracy where there is not a free-flow of political information.

••• ——— •••   ••• ——— •••   ••• ——— •••

Clueless At Campaign Headquarters

By: Rosemarie Jackowski / November 3rd, 2008

The following is a mostly true account. Only names and a few minor details have been changed to protect identities.

Last night I received a phone call. It went something like this.

Caller: Hello, my name is Henry. I am calling from campaign headquarters and would like to ask you a few questions.
Me: Will it take very long?
Caller: No.
Me: OK.
Caller: I want to know if you are going to vote for Obama or the other guy.
Me: Which other guy? There are seven others on the ballot.
Caller: Ugh. Are you sure?
Me: Yes. Would you like me to give you their names?
Caller: Yes.
Me: Baldwin, Barr, Calero, Lariva, McCain, Moore, and Nader.
Long pause — silence on the other end of the phone line.
Caller: Hummmmm
Me: How can you be a campaign worker for one candidate if you don't know the other candidates' positions on the issues?
Caller: I like hanging out here.
Me: How do you feel about the 700 billion dollar bail out?
Caller: Oh, that was bad.
Me: Who are you going to vote for in the Congressional race?
Caller: The Democrat, of course.
Me: But he voted for the bailout.
Caller: Really?
Me: What do think about term limits?
Caller: Yes, that would be good.
Me: Then you should not be voting for an incumbent.
Caller: What's an incumbent?

     ••• ——— •••   ••• ——— •••   ••• ——— •••

The conversation concluded with my recommendation that Henry visit some web sites and read some books. I suggested that he read Joshua Frank, Mickey Z, William Blum and some others.

The ultimate responsibility for the outcome of the election is the voter; but, in defense of Henry- the-Campaign-Worker, maybe he is not completely responsible for his lack of information. This phone conversation could have occurred anywhere in the country but it happened in Vermont. In Vermont some newspapers censor out information about some candidates. Being blacklisted by Vermont newspapers is so common that it has become a badge of honor. Many candidates have been 'Naderized' — denied access to the Press.

In addition, some newspapers in the southern part of the State have even refused to insert the Official State Candidates Information Publication. This publication is nonpartisan. It is authorized by Vermont Law (17 V.S.A. 2810-b) and has been paid for by the taxpayers. For many, this publication is the only source of voter information. A computer is a luxury that many cannot afford.

What is the difference between the Democratic-Republican Party and a gang in the hood? The gang in the hood usually limits its harm to the local area. The Dem-Repub Party causes global harm.

2010 Campaign Statement - A Call For Justice And Ethics In Vermont

By: Rosemarie Jackowski / 2010

Vermont State Constitution - Article 4 - Remedy at law secured to all.

"Every person within this state ought to find a certain remedy, by having recourse to the laws, for all injuries or wrongs which one may receive in person, property or character; every person ought to obtain right and justice, freely, and without being obliged to purchase it; completely and without any denial; promptly and without delay; conformability to the laws."

As a member of Veterans for Peace, Chapter 88 I have been a peace advocate. I am a writer and many of my articles are available on the Internet.

I am a mother and grandmother. In the 1970s I founded an organization, Justice for Children. I have spent much time in court and have been a citizen advocate for decades.

The odds against any candidate who is not a Democrat/Republican are insurmountable, but support of third parties and Independents is important. Vermonters deserve a wider choice of candidates.

I have accepted NO campaign contributions. I owe NO political favors.

My global view includes a profound respect for the rule of law. The most important qualification for the office of attorney general is an absolute, unwavering commitment to Justice for all, young and old, rich and poor, victims and also the accused ... no politics, no cronyism, and no excuses.

     ··· ‒‒‒ ···   ··· ‒‒‒ ···   ··· ‒‒‒ ···

It is the attorney general's office that is the gateway to justice, not only in criminal matters but also in civil cases. When a citizen is injured or killed by the state, it is the office of the attorney general that represents the government and opposes the injured citizen in court. In 1990 the Vermont legislature dropped insurance on state dump trucks, snowplow vehicles, and state cars. *"Self insurance"* by the government places an unreasonable burden on the injured. Any injured citizen is now up against the full force of the government. No citizen can equal the State with its tons of money, teams of lawyers, and access to the bought-and-paid-for testimony of *"expert witnesses"*. In Vermont courts, it is too often money, not the facts, that determines the outcome of the case. Every citizen is at risk. Many people believe that *"it"* can't happen to them — until it does.

How many citizens have had disputes with the government about a highway going through their dining room, or an airport runway going through their yard? How many have had problems with toxins in the workplace?

There are lingering questions about the shooting in the Brattleboro church. Robert Woodward was shot to death by the police. Many believe that Woody and his family never received justice.

I ask only that each voter talk with a friend or neighbor who has dealt with the Office of the Attorney General and then vote his or her conscience on Election Day.

Bugliosi Is Going
For The Big One

By: Rosemarie Jackowski / August 7th, 2008

Consider the following questions: *"Who is responsible for the deaths of more than 4000 U.S. military and countless innocent Iraqis? Is every war crime worthy of Indictment or should some be given a free pass? Should the accused face justice in an open Court which will send a message to the world and, more importantly, to future U.S. Administrations?"*

In the upcoming election, voters will have the opportunity to change the course of history. Across the country, the office of State Attorneys General will be more important during this election than at any time in the past. County Prosecutors and District Attorneys will also have a significant role to play. The time for War Crimes trials has finally come. We can stop holding our collective breath. The second shoe is about to drop.

The Bush Indictment Project has begun. The difference between Impeachment and Indictment is like the difference between night and day. The call for Impeachment looks like a Sunday School picnic by comparison. Impeachment has its flaws. It trivializes the war crimes. It is better than nothing, but not by much. Impeachment can result in removal from office. The criminal prosecution of George W. Bush could result in a life sentence or the death penalty.

The Bush Indictment Project is not perfect. One of the important criticisms is that it tends to place all of the responsibility for the war and the war crimes on the Executive Branch. That view exonerates the Congress. In fact, only the Congress has the power to declare and finance war. The complicity of the Congress is an important issue that should not be overlooked. The public has excused the Congressional crimes, and has focused only on the Bush Administration. Hopefully History will get it right and report that more Iraqi children were killed during the Clinton Administration than under both Bush Administrations and that always, the Congress has had Constitutional authority to wage or prevent war. Most complicit of all are the voters who put the accused war criminals in office in the first place.

Another deficiency of The Indictment Project is that the deaths of the Iraqis might be overlooked and find no justice in a U.S. Court. Some predict that only U.S. military deaths will be considered. What impression will that leave in the rest of the world? It has been estimated that possibly three million Iraqis have been killed by the U.S. since the bombing started in 1991. Those deaths should not wait for justice in an International Court.

In spite of the obvious flaws, The Indictment Project is supported by many — former Attorney General Ramsey Clark and Vincent Bugliosi among others.

In his book, *The Prosecution of George W. Bush for Murder*, Bugliosi makes a strong case for the prosecution of Bush. Speaking in Venice, California on June 25, 2008, Bugliosi says, "*...I am not going to be satisfied until I see George W. Bush in an American court being tried for first degree murder...*". Bugliosi assures the audience that he has established jurisdiction in all fifty states.

In addition to laying out a convincing legal case, Bugliosi offered his services as Special Prosecutor. That is important for two reasons. First, Bugliosi has an impressive record as a prosecutor. During his career, he prosecuted 106 felony jury trials, and lost only one of them. The second reason, is that voters across the country are concerned about diverting resources from the usual duties of the Offices of the State Attorneys General. With Bugliosi on board, the effect on other prosecutions would be minimized.

The ball is now in the voters' court. No longer is it necessary to bow down to Congress and beg for action. Now the voters have the power. If the voters want justice for all who have died in the war their choice will be made clear at the polls. All voters must inform themselves on the position of the candidates for State Attorney General and District Attorney/Prosecutor in their voting districts.

••• ——— •••   ••• ——— •••   ••• ——— •••

Imagine Nuremberg. Imagine hundreds of indictments all across the country. Approximately one thousand public officials have the legal authorization to bring forth an indictment — fifty State Attorneys General, and nine hundred-fifty county prosecutors. No criminal action can be brought by a private citizen. The citizen's power to act is limited to the voting booth; therefore, the most important vote cast in the upcoming election will be for the candidate who is authorized to take legal action — your State Attorney General.

It is really very simple. Get the facts which are clearly laid out in *The Prosecution of George W. Bush for Murder*. Find a candidate who supports your view. Pull the correct lever. Get the popcorn ready. The war crimes trials will be televised.

There's Got To Be A Better Way To Run A Country

By: Rosemarie Jackowski / November 22nd, 2005

"Think about a system where those who make the laws really understand what it is like to live under those laws. Imagine what it would be like to have a president who actually understood what working for a living was like. Maybe there is no better preparation for the Office of President than having been hungry. Many citizens of the U.S. have experienced severe food shortages but, because of the stigma of poverty, it is a hidden problem. The president and the legislators should have life experiences that would help make them empathetic to the average citizen."

There's got to be a better way to run a country. It is hard to imagine a worse scenario than what has been occurring in Washington. The Democratic/Republican members of the ruling class have messed things up so badly, it will take some creative, out of the box thinking to repair the damage. There is a solution.

One of the roots of the problem is the way in which our leaders are voted into office. The level of corporate control of the government has reached obscene levels. The system is corrupted with so much money that a fair electoral process is no longer possible. There is no way to take the money out of the voting process; therefore, we must take the voting process out of the government. The solution to the problem would be to eliminate voting and replace it with a national lottery. All citizens over the age of 18, or 35 in the lottery for the presidency, would have their names entered. At the appointed time the names of office holders would be drawn. This system would have advantages that are impossible under current law.

Imagine a country where no one felt pressured into voting for the lesser of the evil candidates. Imagine a country where wealth was not a requirement for holding office. Think about a country where ordinary citizens, farmers, factory workers, teachers, clerks,

••• ——— •••   ••• ——— •••   ••• ——— •••

health care workers, work-at-home Mothers, etc. had an equal chance of becoming president as elite members of the wealthy class do.

Think about a system where those who make the laws really understand what it is like to live under those laws. Imagine what it would be like to have a president who actually understood what working for a living was like. Maybe there is no better preparation for the Office of President than having been hungry. Many citizens of the U.S. have experienced severe food shortages but, because of the stigma of poverty, it is a hidden problem. The president and the legislators should have life experiences that would help make them empathetic to the average citizen. In 2004 the system put one wealthy fraternity boy up against another wealthy fraternity boy. Unless you are a member of Skull and Bones you have to admit that selecting a president by lottery would be an improvement.

Arguments could be made against this plan for a New National Lottery. It would not be a perfect system. Even with a lottery, there would be the occasional rich frat boy or sorority girl who could get into office, but the odds of that happening would be reduced enough so that it would not be an important consideration. There are Constitutional issues. There would still be some possibility of corruption of the process. Even with all the drawbacks, it would be an improvement over what we now have. Now we have, what might be, one of the worse of all possible systems.

Even a Benevolent Dictatorship, with emphasis on benevolent, would be better than a government under the control of big business.

One thing is certain. The current system is a Doomsday scenario. Maybe it is time to try something new. If not now, when?

   ••• ––– •••   ••• ––– •••   ••• ––– •••

Never Vote For An Incumbent

By: Rosemarie Jackowski / November 2010

Voting for an incumbent is like going back to the same
dentist who pulled the wrong tooth the last time.

Voting for an incumbent is like going back inside your
camping tent even though you were just bitten by a snake
there.

Voting for an incumbent is like re-marrying your former
spouse even though she cheated on you the last time around.

Voting for an incumbent is like getting in a plane with a pilot
who crashed his aircraft last time he went up.

Voting for the incumbent might mean that you need a
change in your medications....

Voting for the incumbent is like taking your computer back
to the same repair shop, even though last time they told you
that your computer needed a lube and an oil change.

Voting for an incumbent is a vote for *"staying the course"*.

Voting for the incumbent means that you believe that things
can never get any better.

Voting for the incumbent signals the end of all hope.

Voting against all incumbents is the perfect way to achieve
term limits.

Monsanto's Udder Disgrace

By: Rosemarie Jackowski / February 11th, 2008

Some might say that Monsanto is more of a threat than al-Qaida, but I won't say that. I remember the track record of Monsanto when it comes to seeking revenge against anyone who is critical of Monsanto's corporate policies. I won't say that I feel compassion for those who have been injured by Monsanto. I won't say that cows suffer painful mastitis because of injections of Monsanto's BGH.

I won't say that Canadian farmer Percy Schmiester deserves support because of what Monsanto did to him. Schmiester was sued by Monsanto. In fact, so many farmers have been sued by Monsanto that a national hotline was set up to assist them.

I won't say that Monsanto puts profits ahead of the health of all of us. I won't say any of these things because I don't have a legal defense fund sufficient to wage a battle against the giant Monsanto. In this land of free speech, sometimes only those with power and wealth have freedom of speech.

What I will say is that, in my opinion, what Monsanto is doing to Ben & Jerry's is an udder disgrace. Monsanto, known for its strong-arm legal tactics, is opposing the labeling of ice cream. Why would Monsanto want information withheld from consumers? It's all about money. Allowing consumers to have the facts could affect the corporation's bottom line. BGH, otherwise known as Recombinant Bovine Growth Hormone, is a drug developed to increase bovine milk production. Ben & Jerry's is fighting for the right to continue to label ice cream that is made with milk from BGH-free cows.

The food chain is under worldwide assault by U.S. corporations. The Master Race of corporations has seized control of the very essence of life itself. We are now in the age of Genetically Modified Doomsday Seeds. Why has there been no public discussion on who should have control of the planetary gene pool?

I applaud vegans. They have reached a higher moral plane than the rest of us; but even they are at risk of Monsantoitis. They must be vigilant if they want to avoid GMOs and *"Roundup Ready"* soy products.

It must be emphasized that all in this article is just my opinion — no Monsanto Process Servers knocking on my door, please.

I vaguely remember, a few years back, Monsanto ran the most oppressive lobbying campaign in the history of the State of Vermont. The crux of the controversy was the labeling of milk – not exactly nuclear physics or brain surgery. Some citizens and members of the State Legislature thought that it was a good idea to indicate on the label if milk came from cows that had not been injected with Monsanto's money-making BGH. This would allow consumers the freedom to make an informed choice in the super market. Monsanto's position, which was supported by the USDA — no surprise there — was that consumers did not have the right to that information.

The milk labeling controversy — and other corporate practices of Monsanto — have been issues for years. For a while every time I saw my Senator, I would greet him with the same comment, *"Hey Bernie, when are you going to do something about Monsanto?"* Senator Bernie would shake his head and raise his hands in frustration.

I often heard him say that no matter how bad you think things are in Washington, they are really much worse. While the Congress is distracted with growth hormones taken by sports figures, our farm animals are being abused with other hormones. Baseball players have a free choice. Cows don't.

The current attack by the giant Monsanto on our beloved Ben & Jerry's shows the dark underside of the corporate culture. Monsanto should back off. They should keep their drugs out of our cows and keep their hands off our ice cream. Is there nothing sacred? Do they have no shame? This is the stuff of summer time picnics, church socials, and children's birthday parties. Sometimes it is only ice cream that can put a smile on the face of Grandpa. Ice cream — the magic potion that was fed to kids in the old days to soothe painful throats after tonsillectomies.

Giant corporations intent on waging battles against the little guys should chill out. It's time for those corporate execs to feast on some Chunky Monkey or maybe a little Cherry Garcia. It just might be the perfect medicine to soothe the savage beast inside their desolate corporate souls.

Twenty-Seven Reasons To Draft Ralph Nader For President

By: Rosemarie Jackowski / January 21st, 2008

The reasons are . . .

1. Hillary
2. John McCain
3. Seat belts
4. The abuse the Katrina victims by their insurance companies
5. 650,000+ dead Iraqi civilians
6. 3000+ dead U.S. military
7. The Black Budget
8. Torture
9. The CIA
10. Blackwater
11. Lack of access to Health care which causes the deaths of 45,000 U.S. citizens every year.
12. CNN, ABC, NBC, CBS, FOX, MSNBC
13. Factory farming and franken foods
14. Monsanto
15. The loss of family farms
16. The lack of regulations to restrict predatory practices by the banking and credit card industry
17. The mortgage crisis
18. Global warming
19. The loss of good will toward the U.S. around the world. Ralph could restore the status of the U.S.
20. He is not a Republican.
21. He is not a Democrat.
22. He is not an Empire builder.
23. He would not invade Iran, Cuba, Syria, Venezuela, Finland, Switzerland, Canada, Mexico, or New Zealand.
24. Ralph owes no favors to any corporation.
25. Ralph cannot be bought.
26. Ralph has a long history of quietly working behind the scene to help ordinary people in their struggles against the powerful — such as the time he helped a group of New

Jersey citizens oppose the construction of a floating nuclear power plant off the coast of Atlantic City. Ralph quietly came to Cape May, no fan-fare, no political motives. He helped the people. The people won. The floating nuclear plant was not built.

27. Ralph is smart, incorruptible, and honest.

Ralph is not the only candidate who should be considered for the presidency. There are others who are also qualified, such as Dennis Kucinich, Angela Davis, Cynthia McKinney, Ward Churchill, William Blum, Cindy Sheehan, and many, many more.

Thinking Outside The (Christmas) Box

By: Rosemarie Jackowski / December 14th, 2007

You say that Christmas has become too commercialized. In some towns the display of decorated trees is now controversial. Confused about whether to say *"Merry Christmas"* or *"Happy Holidays"*. What about Kwanza, Hanukkah, and the Holy Days of Islam? Maybe a simple greeting of *"Peace to you brother"* would be appropriate. Better be careful though with that one. I have a few friends who have been arrested for saying *"Peace"* at the wrong time in the wrong place. Ah, the stress of it all could drive a person to over-indulge in the spiked nog.

It is just a matter of priorities. On a scale of one to ten, the importance of the holiday conundrum is less than zero. The debate of clear lights versus colored lights makes as much sense as arguing the virtues of vanilla versus chocolate ice cream.

The Christmas controversy gets even more intense for those who have children. Many parents find themselves in a no-win situation. Should your child be the only one in the class who does not get a pile of gifts. Will the mental health of children be affected if they are on the leading edge of the controversy; on the other hand, it might be an opportunity to teach a child that being part of the group is not always the best thing. Maybe it is better to minimize the influence of the culture on youthful minds. There is no better time of year to expose the negative side of consumerism.

Where do agnostics and atheists fit in — and others whose belief systems do not allow them to partake in the festivities. Often non-Christians feel abused during this season. It would help if everyone showed respect for everyone else's beliefs and non-beliefs. Kindness and humility require that no one impose his belief system on another.

What about the Christmas story — the virgin birth — the bright star in the East. Some people love it; others are offended by it. No matter what your stand on this controversy, the fact is that the Christmas story has always been a story about a homeless family being bullied by their government. For those who are offended by other details of the events in Bethlehem, there is an updated version of the Holiday story.

Think about the fable of Jose' and Maria. Forced out of their homeland by the trade policies of the powerful government to the north, Jose' and Maria left their tiny village in search of a better life. They traveled in their old sputtering Buick, filled with the hope that they would get jobs and send money back to their families at home.

Jose' and Maria successfully crossed the border but found that there were no jobs for *"people like them"* — people without the proper documents. Jose' was an experienced carpenter. He had helped build the big new Wal-mart in his native village. Now, because of the mortgage meltdown, no builders in the United States were hiring.

Maria was a nurse. She had worked in a hospital. Now she hoped for a job — any kind of job. Her heart was set on getting a housekeeping job at a Holiday Inn — back breaking work, but the promise of a paycheck gave the young couple reason to hope.

Jose' and Maria were running out of money. The transmission in their old car was making strange noises. The weather had turned cold. As they traveled north, they discussed their options. Should they try to make it to the Canadian border where they might be less likely to encounter ICE officials? They could cross into Canada at one of the unmanned border crossings in Vermont; but they would need a miracle to make it that far north.

Maybe they should head for Florida. With a little luck they could pass themselves off as Cubans. Immigrants from Cuba are welcomed in the United States. Jose' and Maria often talked about how differently they were treated because they were Mexican and not Cuban. It wasn't their fault that they were born in Nuevo Lorado rather than Havana.

     ··· ▬▬▬ ···   ··· ▬▬▬ ···   ··· ▬▬▬ ···

It was getting dark and cold. Now to add to the distress, Maria was feeling the first pangs of labor pains. They knew that they could not go to a hospital. They did not have enough money for a motel. Jose' made a sharp left hand turn and pulled into a truck stop.

He parked along side of one of the big rigs. A layer of snow now covered the ground. They had never seen snow before. Maria was fascinated by the peaceful beauty of the glittering flakes as they tumbled down in the beam of the large lights in the parking lot.

After a few hours, Maria's pain was getting unbearable. Tears were streaming down her cheeks as she moaned. Jose' was trembling with fear. He got out of the car and pounded on the door of the rig. After what seemed to be a long time, the door flung open. The largest man that Jose' had ever seen stood there. He was dressed in denim jeans and a rumpled plaid flannel shirt. His long gray beard seemed to be collecting snow flakes as he barked something that was unintelligible. Jose' pointed to his car. Maria was now in the back seat. When the truck driver noticed the woman in the back of Jose's car, his mood changed. He immediately understood the problem. His stern voice softened. He mumbled something about being a Grandpa.

Maria was helped into the cab of the truck. The bed in the sleeper section behind the driver's seat was the site of the miracle. It was there that Maria gave birth to a beautiful baby. With the truck driver's help, Jose' swaddled the newborn in a blanket.

The young couple thanked their new friend for his help and they were on their way. No one is sure whether Jose' headed for Florida or drove north to the Canadian border. It is rumored that on cold winter nights when the stars are just right, the shadow of an old Buick is sometimes seen crossing the Vermont border at Derby Line into Quebec.

••• ––– •••   ••• ––– •••   ••• ––– •••

Hi-Tech Torture

By: Rosemarie Jackowski / November 21st, 2007

> *"...Now the U.S. military directorate charged with developing non-lethal weapons, which has invested more than a decade developing the Active Denial System (ADS), has launched a concerted effort to convince both the public and its own bosses at the defence department of the device's merits.*
>
> *With brand new technology like this, perception is everything," said Col Kirk Hymes, a former Marine artillery officer who heads the directorate.*
>
> *He added that tests were almost complete and the first ADS, also known as the Silent Guardian, could be deployed early next year if the Pentagon allows. The decision is so sensitive that it is expected to be made personally by the defence secretary, Robert Gates, who sent senior representatives to the demonstrations..."*
>
> *– The Telegraph*, November 19th, 2007

Just when it seems that things cannot get any worse, we learn that U.S. military commanders in Iraq are seeking permission to use a new weapon system. This will be the ultimate torture weapon. Its purpose is to cause excruciating pain, but leave no evidence of wounds on the victim. Imagine this weapon at AbuGhraib or Guantanamo. Imagine this weapon at your local precinct. The Department of Defense has named this weapon system *"Active Denial"*.

Besides torture, this weapon can also be used for crowd control — a ray gun which could literally make blood boil. It is based on the same technology as a microwave oven. The human body is comprised mostly of water... think of the sensation of boiling blood. The purpose of this weapon system is to cause an unbearable level of pain so that the victim will submit to the will of the U.S. military or police.

     ••• ——— •••   ••• ——— •••   ••• ——— •••

The gun produces a 95-gigahertz microwave beam that is designed to penetrate 1/64th of an inch. Hummmm, should the experts be trusted to achieve zero defects with a technology that requires so precise a tolerance?

Raytheon, with headquarters in Waltham, Mass. is listed as the prime contractor on this project. Raytheon reports sales of $20.3 billion in 2006. The development of torture devices brings high profits to the corporation. Profits before people seems to be the accepted practice in the United States.

This project brings to mind some questions. The Raytheon web site states that this weapon will be used for *"civilian law enforcement"*. Is this system being designed for domestic use against U.S. citizens? Will it be used for *"crowd control"* at sites of labor disputes and strikes? Will it be coming soon to a war protest near you? Will it be used at the borders to prevent immigration? Does International Law prohibit the use of this weapon on the battlefield? Will the government hide behind Sovereign Immunity when a citizen is injured or killed by this weapon? How will this weapon effect children? Will the NRA lobby for access to this weapon? How will it affect the performance of an implanted medical device, such as a pacemaker?

The bad news is that this weapon is now operational. The good news is that the weapon system has had some major design problems. The designers have failed to realize that a person is not a potato. Microwaving a human to the exact degree of doneness is proving to be problematic. Is there anyone out there who wants to volunteer as a subject for any further field tests that may be required? What they need is a test subject, with a pacemaker, contact lenses, a lot of amalgam dental fillings, and maybe a few metal surgical staples from an old appendectomy. Will they pay a bonus if the subject is pregnant? When the experiment is completed, if the subject is incapacitated, but still alive with no visible wounds, the field test is a success.

Fifty-one million dollars have already been spent on this weapon system. This gun has killed before the trigger was even pulled. In the U.S., 45,000 die each year because of the lack of health care. If that 51 million dollars had been used to provide health care to our fellow citizens many lives would have been saved. The real enemies of the American people are those whose priorities are so warped that they allocate money for ray guns while ignoring the humanitarian needs of the populace.

The design and production of redundant weapon systems is pushed by the lobbying efforts of the arms manufacturers who have been doing a land-office business. Somehow all of this seems to be OK with the employees of Raytheon. The argument that, *"We need the jobs"*, is an old one that has been used to justify the development of the most horrific weapons. It is puzzling that the psyche of so many U.S. workers allows them to be engaged in the design and manufacture of a weapon system designed to torture. As the U.S. economy disintegrates, more will be willing to sell their souls for the pay check at the end of the week.

Will those in the legal community speak out against this hi-tech torture system? Its legality under international law is questionable — but then compliance with international law is not a high priority in the U.S.

Will church leaders give sermons about hi-tech torture? It does not seem to be a hot topic among the clergy.

Will shareholders dump their Raytheon stock? Does Wall Street have a conscience — dumb question, I know.

Will U.S. taxpayers object to having their money used to make weapons of torture? They don't seem to object to cluster bombs, land mines, or nukes.

Will U.S. citizens be duped by the spin of the Pentagon and State Department into thinking that this is just another *"nice"* weapon that we need to *"protect our freedom"*? The propaganda campaign has already begun. Col. Kirk Hymes is quoted as saying, *"With brand new technology like this, perception is everything."*

Waterboarding is low-tech torture. Active Denial is hi-tech torture. Torture is torture no matter how it is done. Most people — with the exception of at least one Justice on the Supreme Court — understand that. Torture by any other name is still torture.

A Death On Valentine Street

By: Rosemarie Jackowski / November 19th, 2007

Frank did not know many people in his small New England town. Frank was old — probably in his 80s. He lived alone in a tiny apartment on Valentine Street.

I don't recall ever meeting him in person, but he told me that we had met once. He started to call me on the phone shortly after there were some news reports about my arrest for protesting the war. He continued to call me on a regular basis for several years. If I did not hear from him for a few weeks, I would make a check-up phone call to make sure that he was OK.

His gentleness was apparent even over the phone wires. His intelligence was also apparent. He spoke in a way that only a well-educated, well-traveled person could. I sometimes wondered if he had a secret past. Maybe he was a retired CIA operative, or more likely maybe he was a retired doctor or psychologist. He was usually too modest to talk much about himself.

He had lived in Washington during the Watergate era and had a passion for facts about the Watergate Break-in. He held on to his big dream. He was determined to find a publisher for a book about Watergate that he planned to write. I admired his willingness to hang on to an old dream even though the odds were stacked against him.

When finances made it necessary for him to give up his television set and his only contact with the outside world was a radio and a telephone, he remained optimistic. He never once complained. When I would ask him if he had eaten that day, he always said yes and then he would tell me not to worry about him.

I often planned to visit him, but something more urgent always came up and prevented it. The visit that I planned was never made. Last Friday I read Frank's name in the Obituary Column. My friend on Valentine Street was dead. The newspaper listed his name as

Celestine Velkas, but to me he was 'Frank'. I assume that he died alone — just as he had lived in the last years of his life — alone in his tiny apartment.

When I called the funeral home to check on the arrangements, I was told that his body had already been cremated. Now, I would not even be able to place a single red rose in his casket.

There is sadness when any fellow human being dies alone. There is even greater sadness when so many in small towns and large cities live their final years in isolation. Some are virtually alone in nursing homes with no one to visit them even on special days. Some, like my friend, are invisible — hidden away in tiny apartments.

How ironic it is, that the nation that thinks of itself as the most compassionate, has so many who live in isolation. Other countries seem to be far more sensitive to the needs of the elderly — and the young. As a society, we in the United States have a lot to learn.

Coming Soon To A Protest Near You; A Weapon System To Make Your Blood Boil

By: Rosemarie Jackowski / August 8th, 2005

"This is the ultimate crowd control weapon. The ray gun could literally make your blood boil. It is based on the same technology as a microwave oven."

Just when it seems that things cannot get any worse, we learn that, despite set backs, the Pentagon is still pursuing the development of its new microwave gun. This will be the ultimate torture weapon. Its purpose is to cause excruciating pain, but leave no evidence of wounds on the victim. Imagine this weapon at AbuGhraib or Guantanamo. Imagine this weapon at your local precinct. The Department of Defense has named this weapon system *"Project Sheriff"*.

This is the ultimate crowd control weapon. The ray gun could literally make your blood boil. It is based on the same technology as a microwave oven. The human body is comprised mostly of water... think of the sensation of boiling blood. The purpose of this weapon system is to cause an unbearable level of pain so that the victim will submit to the will of the *"Sheriff"*.

The gun produces a 95-gigahertz microwave beam that is designed to penetrate only 1/64th of an inch. Hummmm, should the experts be trusted to achieve zero defects with a technology that requires so precise a tolerance?

This project brings to mind some questions. Is this system being designed primarily for domestic use against U.S. citizens? Will it be used for *"crowd control"* at sites of labor disputes and strikes? Will it be coming soon to a war protest near you? Will it be used at the borders to prevent immigration? Does International Law prohibit the use of this weapon on the battlefield? Will the government hide

 ••• ––– •••   ••• ––– •••   ••• ––– •••

behind Sovereign Immunity when a citizen is injured or killed by this weapon? How will this weapon effect children? Will the NRA lobby for access to this weapon? How will it affect the performance of an implanted medical device, such as a pacemaker?

The good news is that the Pentagon is having some major design problems. The designers have failed to realize that a person is not a potato. Microwaving a human to the exact degree of doneness is proving to be problematic. Is there anyone out there who wants to volunteer as a subject for the field tests? What they need is a test subject, with a pacemaker, contact lenses, a lot of amalgam dental fillings, and maybe a few metal surgical staples from an old appendectomy. Will they pay a bonus if the subject is pregnant? When the experiment is completed, if the subject is incapacitated, but still alive with no visible wounds, the field test is a success.

Fifty-one million dollars has already been spent on this weapon system. This gun has killed before the trigger was even pulled. In the U.S., 45,000 die each year because of the lack of health care. If that 51 million had been used to provide health care to our fellow citizens many lives would have been saved. The real enemies of the American people are those whose priorities are so warped that they allocate money for ray guns while ignoring the humanitarian needs of the populace.

The Pentagon, with the help of Congress, has become like a gluttonous dinner guest demanding just one more pork chop. The military wants just one more weapon system, even though it already has enough firepower and nuclear power to kill every living thing on the planet. The voracious appetite of the Department of Offense will continue until the people rise up and say, *"Enough, not one more dollar."*

Raytheon, with headquarters in Waltham, Mass. is listed as the prime contractor on this project. It is the ultimate irony, that Raytheon lists on its web site a memo for having received an award for ethics.

The design and production of redundant weapon systems is pushed by the lobbying efforts of the arms manufacturers who have been doing a land-office business. Somehow all of this seems to be OK with the employees of Raytheon and the other arms dealers. The argument that, *"We need the jobs"*, is an old one that has been used to justify the development of the most horrific weapons.

The blood of victims of U.S. aggression falls upon all of us... taxpayers, engineers, designers, all of us who are involved directly or indirectly in the production of weapons. The time has come to say, *"Enough, not one more new weapon system. Not one more dollar for offense. Not one more death"*. The political will of the citizens of the U.S. has been paralyzed by propaganda and a false sense of patriotism. If the rest of the world wants to be saved from U.S. expansionism, outside intervention will be required. How many others will step up and close ranks with President Rafael Correa?

9/11 — Conspiracy Or Blowback?

By: Rosemarie Jackowski / September 8th, 2007

It is now time to look back and remember — well not exactly. That's what we have been doing for what seems like forever. We are a nation that is stuck in grief and frightened of the future. GWB has used the words *"nine eleven"* more times than he has said, *"Laura, where's the remote."*

Now it is time for a reality check so we can finally end the denial. 9/11 was the result of blowback. They did it to us because of what we had been doing to them for decades. Sooner or later every school yard bully gets pay back. Serious and tragic as 9/11 was, the number of deaths does not even compare with the deaths that have resulted from U.S. interventions.

Author/historian William Blum states:
"Between 1945 and 2005 the United States has attempted to overthrow more than 40 foreign governments, and to crush more than 30 populist-nationalist movements struggling against intolerable regimes… In the process, the U.S. caused the end of life for several million people, and condemned many millions more to a life of agony and despair." (Rogue State: A Guide to the World's Only Superpower).

"No matter how paranoid or conspiracy-minded you are, what the government is actually doing is worse than you imagine" (ibid).

Many believe the 9/11 conspiracy theories — understandable, since it is so well known that this government is not above the killing of its own. Whether the government was the cause or not, it surely has taken full advantage of the tragedy. The main challenge to the conspiracy theorists comes from Osama Bin Laden. He explained why the attack occurred. Anybody remember his statement? He gave three reasons — the unfair treatment of the Israeli/Palestinian issue, the stationing of U.S. troops in their holy land, and the sanctions which resulted in the deaths of a half million Iraqi children. Thank you for setting the record straight, Osama. Notice he did not say that they attacked us because of our *"freedoms"*. He did not say that they attacked us because of religious differences. Most of those who are informed about U.S. foreign policy knew the reasons for the attack even before Osama made his statement.

The 9/11 Commission Report leaves a lot to be desired. It has raised the art of obfuscation to new heights. I confess — I have not read all 567 pages of the Report. After the first three pages, I ran out of NoDoz. I did watch the Congressional Hearings on C-Span. In her testimony before the Congressional Committee, Kristen Breitweiser said, *"...The jigs up..."* (C-Span2, Aug. 17, 2004, 10:45 a.m.). It would have been a move in the right direction if she had been referring to U.S. actions around the world, but the context of her statement showed that she believes that the tragedy of 9/11 was a failure of Intelligence. The testimony of other family members of victims, Stephen Push and Mary Fetchet, indicated a greater willingness to recognize that 9/11 was a failure of U.S. foreign policy and diplomacy. In Mary Fetchet's testimony, she stated, *"...Foreign policy is the core of the threat of terrorism..."* Fetchet's statement might be the single most important comment ever made about 9/11.

The most compassionate act, that any of us can do in support of the 9/11 families, is to inform others about the government's international policies that led to 9/11. Has any member of Congress or any member of the commission mentioned the connection between U.S. foreign policy and the 9/11 attacks? Yes, Ron Paul made the shocking 9/11-foreign policy connection during a recent Republican debate. Paul's statement almost sent Giuliani into a seizure.

Ignoring the role that U.S. foreign policy played in causing the tragedy of 9/11 is like ignoring the elephant in the middle of the room. Authors have been predicting a 9/11 type of attack for many years. Chalmers Johnson wrote his book, *Blowback*, before the attack happened.

The CIA has been using the term *"blowback"* for decades because they knew that there would be a violent reaction to U.S. foreign policy. It was common knowledge. In view of this, how can it be that not one of our elected officials in Washington could foresee the event? There are two possibilities: none of our representatives was smart enough to think in terms of cause and effect. That is hard to believe. There is a better explanation. Some members of Congress did know. They did not know the time and place of the attack, but they had to know that an attack would be the inevitable result of U.S. foreign policy. If they didn't know it before 9/11, they surely have to know it now, and that brings us up to today and the ongoing presidential campaign season.

Dennis Kucinich says that he is opposed to the U.S. Mid-East policies and the war. Why are there no other candidates, with the possible exception of Ron Paul, suggesting that the time has come for a major change in U.S. foreign policy? Neither Kucinich or Paul stands much chance of winning the Primary. Both share a fatal flaw. They are members of the major political parties and that indicates an acceptance of what these two Parties have done in recent years. Any candidate who is not in agreement with the Party Platform, should run as an Independent. A vote for any Democrat or Republican signals an acceptance of the deadly policies that led to 9/11. It is time to think outside the box and look at candidates from alternative parties. It was during the Clinton administration that Madeleine Albright stated that the death of 500,000 children was worth it. It's a toss-up when trying to decide which Party is more dangerous. Both Parties have betrayed the people in favor of the war profiteers who wander the halls of Congress.

The biggest flaw in the conspiracy theory is that it ignores the anger that has built up in the rest of the world — anger that is a direct result of U.S. actions. 9/11 was not acceptable but it was predictable and understandable — a simple application of the Law of Cause and Effect. Who caused 9/11? Well maybe it really was the government after all. Nineteen men hijacked the planes, but the ultimate cause was the policies of the government of the United States.

The provocative policies continue. The Pentagon has just released a list of 1200 targets to bomb in Iran. Was this announcement a well-planned, deliberate act designed to provoke another attack? A new 9/11 attack would further enrich the corporations that manufacture weapons. Just follow the money since the first 9/11. 9/11 is the goose that has laid the golden grenade.

Is there an ongoing conspiracy to create blowback? Maybe the conspiracy theorists have a point.

A Perfect Storm In Medical Care

By: Rosemarie Jackowski / August 20th, 2007

An Associated Press report reminds me of a poem that my father had hanging on the wall in his garage. The framed print said, *"From the time you were born till you ride in a hearse, things are never so bad that they couldn't get worse."* My Dad was a very wise man. The poem that inspired him many years ago says a lot about the health care system today in the United States.

> On August 18, 2007, the AP reported:
> …Medicare will stop paying the costs of treating infections, falls, objects left in surgical patients and other things that happen in hospitals that could have been prevented….The rule identifies eight conditions _ including three serious types of preventable incidents sometimes called *"never events"* _ that Medicare no longer will pay for. Those conditions are: objects left in a patient during surgery; blood incompatibility; air embolism; falls; mediastinitis, which is an infection after heart surgery; urinary tract infections from using catheters; pressure ulcers, or bed sores; and vascular infections from using catheters. The Centers for Medicare and Medicaid Services said it also would work to add three more conditions to the list next year….Last year, Mark McClellan, then director of the Medicare and Medicare programs, said the government could save hundreds of millions of dollars a year if the Medicare program stopped paying for medical errors such as operations on the wrong body part or mismatched blood transfusions. Medicare provides coverage for about 43 million elderly and disabled people…

The implications of this new rule will have disastrous effects for many — young and old. The scenario is this: you go to hospital for a minor surgical procedure — maybe an appendectomy. When you are wheeled out of surgery, you are minus one appendix and in its place you have a pair of surgical gloves, three sponges, and a spit sink. Weeks later the infection created by the foreign objects causes your temperature to approach the boiling point of tar. You return to your medical provider. X-rays diagnose the problem. Based on the new Medicare rules, the hospital denies care. The patient dies.

Conspiracy theorists might come to the conclusion that this new set of rules was planned a while back. The path was prepared. The propaganda campaign about the ease of filing and winning medical malpractice suits made way for these new Medicare rules. Tort reformists have poisoned not only the national jury pool, but also the national psyche. We now have a Perfect Storm in medical care. When a patient is the victim of medical malpractice he is on his own. There will be no medical coverage for alleviating medical errors. To make matters worse, the possibility of achieving justice in the courts is almost less than zero.

The continuing stream of bad news about health care could be sugarcoated by remembering that there are many excellent surgeons and other medical practitioners. That fact is not debated. Many years ago, after walking around with a ruptured appendix for a considerable length of time, my life was saved by a surgeon. I will never forget Dr. John Groblewski — a talented and dedicated doctor in Pennsylvania. He was loved by his many patients. Unfortunately, the new Medicare ruling will taint all doctors, even the good ones. Why are they silent?

Those who can afford it will join with many who leave the United States as medical tourists. They can have their surgery done in places like India, Thailand, South Africa, and Costa Rica. For those without money, medical care in the U.S. will continue to be a crapshoot.

   ··· ––– ···   ··· ––– ···   ··· ––– ···

Jose Padilla — Just A Nice Kid From Brooklyn

By: Rosemarie Jackowski / August 18th, 2007

How did a nice kid from Brooklyn end up like this — arrested and imprisoned. He was subjected to the most inhumane torture for more than three years, then tried, and convicted. Now he faces a possible life sentence. What did he do, what crime did he commit? How many people did he murder? None, zero, nada, not even one. He never injured anyone.

The June 14, 2002 issue of *Time* named Padilla, Person of the week. *"Padilla entered public life via an announcement from Moscow on Monday, by Attorney General John Ashcroft, that an al-Qaeda operative had been captured at Chicago's O'Hare International Airport, en route to contaminate a U.S. city with a radiological bomb. Within minutes panicky cable news channels were running file footage of mushroom clouds. They then spent much of the next two days atoning via a more sober explanation of dirty-bomb scenarios — and why they're not nearly as scary as they sound . . ."*

Padilla's crime was that he lacked a PR representative who could discredit the propaganda that the government was using against him. He needed an agent. Celebrities use them every time they get into trouble.

Government prosecutors took steps to make sure that Jose Padilla became known as the *"Dirty Bomber."* The intensity of the government smear campaign against Padilla would have made Mother Teresa look like a mass murderer. Padilla was tried and convicted in the press long before his trial in court. In fact, Padilla never had a bomb. He never had the materials necessary to build a bomb.

A jury decision is only as good as the information upon which it is based. Too often, the most important evidence is withheld from the jury. Political viewpoints and personal prejudices of jurors are often more important than the facts of the case. The August 17, 2007 *Concord Monitor* reports that Peter Whoriskey of the *Washington Post* states, *"…The jury did seem to be an oddly cohesive group. On the last day of trial before the July 4th holiday, jurors arranged to dress in shirts so that each row in the jury box was its own patriotic color — red, white or blue. . ."*

In the Padilla case, did the jury know that the defendant was the victim of extreme torture for more than 3 years? That information might have made the jury sympathetic toward Padilla. On the August 16, 2007 broadcast of *Democracy Now*, forensic psychiatrist, Dr. Angela Hegarty, stated that, *"What happened at the brig was essentially the destruction of a human being's mind. Padilla's personality was deconstructed and reformed."* She said the effects of the extreme isolation on Padilla are consistent with brain damage. *"I don't know if he's guilty or not of the charges that they brought against him,"* said Dr. Hegarty. *"But . . . he's already paid a tremendous price for his trip to the Middle East."*

This case has important legal implications for all of us, our children and grandchildren. Legal history is made every day but this case is different. If something like this can happen to a U.S. citizen — a good kid from Brooklyn, it can happen to anybody. Jose Padilla today, Johnny Jones tomorrow. Yes, Jose was at one time a member of a street gang — so were millions of other young men and women.

The Courts in the United States leave a lot to be desired and this case proves that it is time to clean up the judicial system, end torture, and shut down the secret prison system. In addition reparations should be paid to Padilla for the years that he suffered extreme torture at the hands of the U.S. government.

In the meantime, there is not a better case that is crying out to be made into a movie. It has it all — intrigue, secret prisons, violence, and torture. Hollywood are you listening? This is a film that might result in saving a life. The life that is saved might be yours.

Iraqi Order 81 Update :: It Is Even Worse Than Originally Reported ::

By: Rosemarie Jackowski / August 12th, 2005

"Prior to the U.S. invasion, agriculture in Iraq was flourishing. The Fertile Crescent had developed a system of farming that was the envy of the world. Now, under Occupation, centuries of progress have been destroyed, almost overnight."

On August 8, 2005 Reuters reported that the Iraqi seed supply is at risk. Below is an excerpt from the Reuters report.

"... The war in Iraq destroyed the country's seed industry, putting the country's domestic food supply at risk, the United Nations food agency said on Monday as it appealed for aid to rebuild farming."

The Food and Agriculture Organization said it needed $5.4 million to help the agriculture ministry rebuild a seed industry destroyed by the fighting and looting.

"Iraq had a relatively stable and functioning public-sector-controlled seed industry before the war in 2003. After the war, research and seed production facilities have greatly deteriorated," FAO said in a statement.

"Iraq can now cover only 4 percent of its demand for quality seeds from its own resources...."

"If no immediate action is taken, serious seed shortages can be expected in the near future, threatening the country's food security...."

How convenient...perfect timing. What a break for U.S. corporations, such as Monsanto. First outlaw the seeds and then destroy them, or did it happen the other way around. Were the seeds destroyed first and then outlawed? This news story has thus far received very little attention.

••• ——— •••   ••• ——— •••   ••• ——— •••

The news story about the Iraqi Orders has been virtually ignored by the U.S. press. Order 81 is just one of 100 Orders that have been imposed on the people of Iraq by the U.S. government. These orders are sometimes referred to as the Bremmer Orders. No one in the U.S. or Iraq was ever allowed to cast a vote in the ballot box for any of these Orders. This says a lot about the kind of democracy that the U.S. is imposing on the people of Iraq.

The important information about Iraqi Order 81 is that it was designed to have a major impact on the way farming is done in Iraq. This order prohibits Iraqi farmers from using the methods of agriculture that they have used for centuries. The practice of saving seeds from one year to the next is now illegal in Iraq. Order 81 wages war on Iraqi farmers. They have lost the freedom to choose their own methods of agriculture. The legalese in which the orders are written creates confusion about their exact meaning, but the desired result is obvious. Order 81 prohibits the farmers from using their own seeds, on their own farms, to grow their own crops.

Prior to the U.S. invasion, agriculture in Iraq was flourishing. The Fertile Crescent had developed a system of farming that was the envy of the world. Now, under Occupation, centuries of progress have been destroyed, almost overnight.

The food chain has been under worldwide assault by U.S. corporations for some time now. The Master Race of corporations has seized control of the very essence of life itself. We are now in the age of Genetically Modified Doomsday Seeds. The USDA was complicit in the development of these bastard seeds.

This is not a new phenomenon. It has been a gradual takeover. Remember Percy Schmeiser, the Canadian farmer, who was sued by Monsanto? Not enough people stood up for Percey, so then they came for other farmers. In fact, Monsanto has sued so many farmers that a national hotline (1-888-FARMHLP) has now been set up to assist them.

Is it possible that Iraqi farmers think back fondly to the good old days before the Occupation and before Order 81? Even Saddam Hussein allowed them to save seeds for the next year's crop. Is the Pentagon a worse master than Saddam?

Farmers and consumers around the world need to stand in solidarity with the farmers and consumers in Iraq. There is no one who contributes more to society than the farmer. At the top of that hierarchy is the organic farmer. Doctors, lawyers, plumbers, and factory workers make important contributions to society, but none would survive without the farmer.

Why did the U.S. destroy the seeds? Did the Pentagon mistake the seeds for bombs and WMD's? Think of that as a headline for tomorrow's paper, *"CIA confuses pomegranate seeds with WMD's."* This sounds like a comedy *"headline"* from the Leno show. If the survival of thousands of people was not an issue, we could all laugh at the absurdity of this saga. The propagandists will try to convince the world that the destruction of the Iraqi seeds was just a mistake, an accident of war...collateral damage. Iraqi Order 81 proves otherwise. Iraqi Order 81 is proof that the U.S. had a strategic plan which would insure that U.S. corporations would not have to compete with the Iraqi farmers. U.S. corporations don't like competition. The idea of free markets is just a myth. The Predatory Capitalism of the U.S. could not survive without the threat of the military behind it.

Can it be denied that U.S. corporations are seeking total control of the food supply of the planet? After all of the seeds that are owned by farmers are destroyed, it will be necessary for the farmers to purchase them. Those most likely to profiteer are U.S. seed companies. General Smedley Butler was right. War is still a racket.

Imagine what would happen if there was a successful worldwide movement of resistance, an international Save the Seed Campaign. A source in Australia reports that a seed bank has been set up there. Every other nation must heed this warning and set up secure seed banks. It is not known what the U.S. government will do to eliminate this competition to U.S. seed corporations. Will the countries that institute seed banks be on a Pentagon hit list? Another possibility will be a covert CIA operation.

The U.S. policy of using food as a weapon of war shows a depraved, mind numbing level of cruelty. This has been referred to as the Ultimate War Crime. It is one of the most serious Crimes Against Humanity of our generation.

There is a hidden tragedy in this seed destruction policy of the U.S. The U.S. has not only endangered the entire population of Iraq but it has also shot each of its own citizens in the foot. Maybe it has rendered a fatal shot to our children and future generations. No one will ever know if any of the seeds, that have been destroyed during our war and occupation, would have produced plants that could have been used to prevent or cure disease. The seeds that have been lost can never be replaced.

Someday, in the distant future, maybe we will become more civilized. Then we will have monuments to honor farmers. We will have parades in celebration of farm workers. The era of glorification of war will just be a fading memory.

An Open Letter To Congress

Rosemarie Jackowski / January 14th, 2007

Ladies and Gentlemen:

We have a moral crisis unlike any in the history of this nation. Since March 20, 2003 the United States has killed 650,000 Iraqi civilians. This is the number that was accepted at the Congressional Hearing of December 11, 2006. In addition to the 650,000, we must add the 500,000 children who perished because of the illegal U.S. blockade. Also, it must be pointed out that many died in the bombings that started in 1991 and continue today. Some estimate the total number of Iraqi civilian deaths at more than 2 million.

It is indisputable that the number of killed Iraqis is more than one million. This is not *"collateral damage"*. This is a slaughter reminiscent of another time in history.

Ladies and gentlemen, the blood of each of these human beings is on your hands. It may be politically convenient to place all of the blame on the President, but I remind you that only the Congress has the power to declare war. Only the Congress has the power to fund the war. The President has no planes, no bombs, and no tanks. Only the Congress has the power to provide the weapons that have been used in Iraq. If George Bush had to fight a war, his only weapon might be the chain saw that he normally uses on the ranch.

The argument that funding must continue in order to *"protect"* the troops is a false one. The only way to stop the killing is to order an immediate withdrawal of all troops and U.S. civilian contractors. A complete withdrawal is needed, not a redeployment. Redeployment is just a way of saying to the world, *"We won't kill you today, but our guns are near-by, loaded, and ready to fire"*.

The complete withdrawal from Iraq should just be the first step in a new U.S. foreign policy. The total withdrawal of all military troops on foreign soil should be the next step. Chalmers Johnson states that the U.S. has 700 bases in 130 countries. The methods used by the U.S. to acquire some of these bases exposes the U.S. to Charges of genocide. Please review the history of Diego Garcia.

The Iraqi people have been the victims of this illegal war. Many who have died are women, children and the elderly. I urge you to look at the war photos as collected by Robert Fisk. Ladies and Gentlemen of the Congress, that is what you have done. You have blown the heads off children. To you, I say, *"Shame"*. You have brought shame not only on yourselves, but on all of us - taxpayers, voters, and ordinary U.S. citizens. The whole world knows what you and we have done. The whole world is watching to see what you and we will do next.

     ••• ——— •••   ••• ——— •••   ••• ——— •••

Vermont Vets Support Ward Churchill Statement

By: Rosemarie Jackowski / June 20th, 2006

Veterans for Peace, Chapter 88, held its monthly meeting in Vermont on June 11, 2006. The members agreed by consensus that the following quote would be supported and endorsed. The quote appeared on the blog site http://www.mickeyz.net on June 9, 2006. The statement was made by Ward Churchill and is taken from Derrick Jensen's book, *Endgame.*

> *"What I want is for civilization to stop killing my people's children. If that can be accomplished peacefully, I will be glad. If signing a petition will get those in power to stop killing Indian children, I will put my name at the top of the list. If marching in a protest will do it, I'll walk as far as you want. If holding a candle will do it, I'll hold two. If singing protest songs will do it, I'll sing whatever songs you want me to sing. If living simply will do it, I will live extremely simply. If voting will do it, I'll vote. But all of those things are allowed by those in power, and none of those things will ever stop those in power from killing Indian children. They never have, and they never will. Given that my people's children are being killed, you have no grounds to complain at whatever means I use to protect the lives of my people's children. And I will do whatever it takes."* -Ward Churchill

Speaking only for myself and not the other members of VFP, I make the observation that many in VFP are total pacifists, some are not. Some are Democrats, others are not. Some participate in partisan politics, others do not. Some are totally committed to non-violence, others accept resistance by any means necessary to stop aggression. To have any group with such a full range of political views endorse any statement is quite a process. The members of Chapter 88 who were involved in the discussion of the Churchill statement are an exceptional group ... mostly old vets who possess a firm commitment to dedicating their lives to working for global peace and justice. Each member put forth his/her argument with skill, passion, and an admirable level of emotion.

One member suggested that the statement be changed to include ALL children, not only Indian children. That suggestion was rejected because the authenticity of the statement would then be compromised and it would not be a Churchill quote. For those who are troubled by the reference to *"Indian"* children, I say we are all Indian children. We are all Iraqi children. We are all American children.

The main point of discussion was predictably the last two sentences, *"Given that my people's children are being killed, you have no grounds to complain at whatever means I use to protect the lives of my people's children. And I will do whatever it takes."* Chapter 88 is a diverse group that includes some pacifists who are deeply offended by any form of violence. The last two sentences troubled those members, but in the end consensus was reached and the statement was endorsed exactly as it was made by Churchill.

The vets in Vermont have now taken a stand. They support the statement intended to protect children from being killed by war and other actions and inactions of those in power. Will the rest of the country catch up with the Vermont vets and also endorse the statement?

When I first saw this Churchill statement on the Mickey Z blog site, my initial reaction was that it was beautifully constructed poetry. Ward Churchill, the gentle poet, that was a new concept. As I read and re-read it over and over, I came to the conclusion that it is one of the most powerful pleas for peace and justice in literature.

     ••• ——— •••   ••• ——— •••   ••• ——— •••

God And The Red Sox

By: Rosemarie Jackowski / October 6th, 2005

"If someone believes that God exists in the sycamore tree on the village square, so what. Does it cause any harm? Belief in the importance of the game requires at least as much blind faith as the belief that God exists in that sycamore tree."

Recently there has been a growing movement criticizing religion. Some of the criticism is valid. Remember the Crusades? Religion, especially organized religion, does not have a perfect track record. Any human activity which is organized in a way that discourages critical thought and careful examination should be subject to the same scrutiny as religion is. That brings up another issue. What about the mindless worship of organized sports teams?

Can anyone explain why it should be considered to be a great human achievement when one team wins over another team? Usually there are only two teams in competition so everyone knows at the start of the game that either team A or team B will win, unless there is a tie. The sports fan is one of the great mysteries of our time and scientific proof that more evolution of the species would be helpful. How can an otherwise rational human place such importance on a spherical object. In the course of human events does it really matter if the basketball goes over the goal post in the outfield and scores a hole-in-one?

OK, OK. You say that sports help the economy by making some people very wealthy. So does war, and I don't like that either. You say that sports activities are good for the youth of the nation because they teach competition. Teaching cooperation would be better. The negative aspects of sports are very troubling. The my-team-is-better-than-your-team mentality leads to the idea that I am better than you and my country is better than yours.

The same rational human beings that make the argument that their team is best often criticize others who say that their religion is the best. Why does it matter if someone has a different religious view? If someone believes that God exists in the sycamore tree on the village square, so what. Does it cause any harm? Belief in the importance of the game requires at least as much blind faith as the belief that God exists in that sycamore tree.

In addition to the above it should be noted that religion has often inspired great acts of benevolence and courage. Remember Ghandi, Dorothy Day, Bishop Oscar Romero, the Berrigan Brothers, Martin Luther King, Malcolm X, and currently the St. Pat's Four. The Quakers have been active in the anti-war movement and always have ongoing charitable projects. The Buddhists, the Amish, and the Mennonites, to mention just a few, all have teachings about peace and charity.

It could be argued that sports are beneficial in a culture because they provide a source of recreation, joy, and pleasure. Joy and pleasure are important, no question about that. Every moment of every day should be filled with joy. That is another reason to criticize sports events. There is almost always a losing team. One group of fans is sure to face disappointment.

The most important reason to question the impact of sports on our culture is the way that sports fans are victims of groupthink. It often appears that they have lost their critical thinking ability. They all march to the same drummer. Maybe someday, after our species has evolved a little more, all competitive sporting events will be eliminated. Then, instead of marching to the same drummer, we will all march to our own full symphonic orchestras.

A Call For Open Borders - Walk Out, Speak Up, Never Give In

By: Rosemarie Jackowski / April 1st, 2006

Congratulations to all of those who have walked out in support of the Mexican Americans who are seeking the freedom to travel across the border. Bienvenidos. Never allow anyone to tell you that you are an *"illegal"* or an *"alien"*. We are all part of the human family. You are our brothers and sisters. We welcome you.

Listening to corporate media and talk shows has exposed a dark underside of the USA culture. Hate-filled, xenophobic speech is filling the airways. FOX news seems to be in a state of panic. Some in the U.S. want the Mexicans to be treated as second-class citizens. Might as well paint a black dot on the forehead of every immigrant.

Our paranoid, racist policy toward Mexicans is apparent to the whole world. The Mexicans should be given at least the same rights as those coming from Cuba. Our borders should be wide open. Welcome stations should be built there to assist the travelers.

One argument being used against immigration is that the inclusion of the Mexicans will lower wages in the U.S. That is like blaming the residents of the Ninth Ward for the failure of the levee system. The purchasing power of wages in the United States has been steadily falling for decades. It has nothing to do with the Mexicans. It has everything to do with the globalization of corporations. Anger should be directed at corporate CEOs and shareholders, not the workers. The fight for a fair wage system must include efforts to globalize the international labor market. To do otherwise ignores the basic facts. The work force needs global standards for wages, benefits, safety, and working conditions.

Opening the borders would bring many advantages. Workers coming from Mexico and other countries would boost the Social Security system by increasing the number of workers. In some U.S. communities the population is decreasing. School systems are experiencing decreasing numbers of students. The new residents would be welcomed in those communities.

There also would be cultural benefits. The U.S. population is deficient in language skills compared to other industrialized nations. This influx from the south could help the U.S. become bilingual. Many in other countries speak three or four languages.

The history of the southern border is relevant today. How did the U.S. acquire that large piece of real estate known as Texas? How much Mexican blood was shed there? We have a debt to pay to our southern neighbors. The least that we should do is either allow the Mexicans to live and work here permanently, or else return Texas to its original owners.

USA Assassination Plots

By: Rosemarie Jackowski / August 28th, 2005

It is reported that on the August 22, 2005 broadcast of The 700 Club, The Reverend Pat Robertson said of Venezuelan President Hugo Chávez:

"...I don't know about this doctrine of assassination, but if he thinks we're trying to assassinate him, I think that we really ought to go ahead and do it. It's a whole lot cheaper than starting a war, and I don't think any oil shipments will stop...."

Here is the list of assassination attempts as compiled by historian William Blum.[1]

- 1949 - Kim Koo, Korean opposition leader
- 1950s - CIA/Neo-Nazi hit list of more than 200 political figures in West Germany to be *"put out of the way"* in the event of a Soviet invasion
- 1950s - Chou En-lai, Prime minister of China, several attempts on his life
- 1950s, 1962 - Sukarno, President of Indonesia
- 1951 - Kim Il Sung, Premier of North Korea
- 1953 - Mohammed Mossadegh, Prime Minister of Iran
- 1950s (mid) - Claro M. Recto, Philippines opposition leader
- 1955 - Jawaharlal Nehru, Prime Minister of India
- 1957 - Gamal Abdul Nasser, President of Egypt
- 1959, 1963, 1969 - Norodom Sihanouk, leader of Cambodia
- 1960 - Brig. Gen. Abdul Karim Kassem, leader of Iraq
- 1950s-70s - José Figueres, President of Costa Rica, two attempts on his life
- 1961 - Francois *"Papa Doc"* Duvalier, leader of Haiti
- 1961 - Patrice Lumumba, Prime Minister of the Congo (Zaire)
- 1961 - Gen. Rafael Trujillo, leader of Dominican Republic
- 1963 - Ngo Dinh Diem, President of South Vietnam

- 1960s-70s - Fidel Castro, President of Cuba, many attempts on his life
- 1960s - Raúl Castro, high official in government of Cuba
- 1965 - Francisco Caamaño, Dominican Republic opposition leader
- 1965-6 - Charles de Gaulle, President of France
- 1967 - Che Guevara, Cuban leader
- 1970 - Salvador Allende, President of Chile
- 1970 - Gen. Rene Schneider, Commander-in-Chief of Army, Chile
- 1970s, 1981 - General Omar Torrijos, leader of Panama
- 1972 - General Manuel Noriega, Chief of Panama Intelligence
- 1975 - Mobutu Sese Seko, President of Zaire
- 1976 - Michael Manley, Prime Minister of Jamaica
- 1980-1986 - Muammar Qaddafi, leader of Libya, several plots and attempts upon his life
- 1982 - Ayatollah Khomeini, leader of Iran
- 1983 - Gen. Ahmed Dlimi, Moroccan Army commander
- 1983 - Miguel d'Escoto, Foreign Minister of Nicaragua
- 1984 - The nine comandantes of the Sandinista National Directorate
- 1985 - Sheikh Mohammed Hussein Fadlallah, Lebanese Shiite leader (80 people killed in the attempt)
- 1991 - Saddam Hussein, leader of Iraq
- 1993 - Mohamed Farah Aideed, prominent clan leader of Somalia
- 1998, 2001-2 - Osama bin Laden, leading Islamic militant
- 1999 - Slobodan Milosevic, President of Yugoslavia
- 2002 - Gulbuddin Hekmatyar, Afghan Islamic leader and warlord
- 2003 - Saddam Hussein and his two sons

Of course the official explanation for all of these assassination attempts is denial.

So maybe Robertson did all of us a big favor. He exposed the dark side of U.S. Foreign Policy. He should receive the praise

    ••• — — — •••   ••• — — — •••   ••• — — — •••

of a grateful nation. His statements could chip away at the misinformation that most of us are wallowing in. We are a nation that has relied on assassination as an integral part of our foreign policy for a very long time. Like it or not, that's the way it is.

Note: [1]. The list of assassination plots was taken from "Killing Hope" by William Blum.

The Bashing Of Bennish

By: Rosemarie Jackowski / March 04th, 2006

It looks like the Press has found another scapegoat. Must be that the Ward Churchill bashing was no longer pulling in the high ratings so now begins the Bashing of Bennish. Jay Bennish is a high school geography teacher at Overland High School in Aurora, Colorado.

Recently one of his students taped some of Bennish's comments during a class. I am not offended that a student would take that action, either on his own or under the direction of someone with less than pure motives. All classrooms should be open to public scrutiny at all times.

A while back in Vermont there was an incident. In the middle of the night the local police chief gained entrance into the high school classroom of a teacher who was an anti-war activist. The chief was on a mission to inspect the classroom bulletin board. He suspected that there might be some anti-war material posted there. *"Can't have none of that there Commie stuff infecting the minds of our youth."*

Anti-war information, anti-capitalist information, anti-government information, anti-military information are now verboten. In other words, we have become an anti-information culture. Any discussion of the important issues is not allowed. No one is allowed to stray too far outside the Democrat/Republican Party Line.

Hannity and Colmes aired their views of the Bennish classroom controversy during their March 2 program. It is not surprising that both Sean and Alan bashed Bennish. *"Fair and balanced"* has never been a view that is held at Fox or MSNBC or CNN. More importantly, fair, balanced, and factual information is also missing from many textbooks currently in use in our government run schools.

What is remarkable is the consistency of the media to engage in ad hominem attacks against anyone who holds an out-of-the-box global view. The folks at Fox really need to get out more. Out here in the real world there are many different global views. Some citizens in this country don't support capitalism. Ain't that a shocker. Some folks even refer to it as *"predatory capitalism"*. Some folks don't support wars of aggression and many do not support the occupation of other countries by this government. Sometimes anti-war activists are tolerated, but anti-capitalist activists, now that is a whole other issue. It strikes at the heart of the Empire.

It is the educational system that has enabled the global aggressions that have inflamed the rest of the world. The Harvard/napalm connection is just one old example of the military-university complex. The failure of our schools to give an accurate view of world history is an even bigger problem that educators often ignore. This is not a freedom of speech issue. It is an issue of the right of students to have access to accurate historical information. Do students have the legal right to accurate historical information?

I applaud Bennish. He is one of the few with the moral fortitude to do the right thing. We should not allow him to be alone in bearing the burden that comes with exposing the truth. If the facts that Bennish presented to his class were wrong, then and only then, should he be criticized. I have yet to hear anyone attack the information he presented to his students. Instead of bashing Bennish, he should be a candidate for *"The Teacher of the Year"* award. The entire country should be examining the lessons that Bennish attempted to teach. A free and open discussion of the information would benefit this *"Mis-informed R us Nation"*.

Unfortunately, this Bennish blip on the media's radar screen will go down as just one more missed opportunity for the press to become informed. It is doubtful that the issues that Bennish bought to his students will ever be addressed in the media in this country.

The recently released Bin Laden tape made a reference to

a book by William Blum. Those in the media who interviewed Blum immediately after the tape was released never seemed to get the point. The serious issues in Blum's books were never discussed and it is doubtful that the information that Bennish tried to give to his students will ever be discussed openly.

Until those in the media are themselves educated enough to discuss the important issues, the ad hominem attacks will continue. Sean and Alan, you really should get out more.

  ••• ——— •••   ••• ——— •••   ••• ——— •••

A Letter To Kate O'Beirne

By: Rosemarie Jackowski / February 20th, 2006

Dear Kate,

Right now I am watching your interview on C-Span Book TV. Thank you for the book, which covers many important topics.

Women Who Make the World Worse contains some valid arguments. There is much in your book that is irrefutable; but during the interview you made a serious mistake. At one point you said that a single mother should look for a father for her children. That statement is evidence of your lack of understanding of the causes of childhood poverty, a leading social problem of our time. It feeds into the myth that these children have no fathers. I need to remind you that there have not been any Immaculate Conceptions in recent years. There is no bright star shining in the East.

Instead of taking time out to look for another man to marry, most single mothers I have known were too busy working two or three jobs to have time even for a bathroom break. Courtship and romance are luxuries that many can only dream about. You are guilty of thinking in-the-box of an economically privileged woman instead of facing the reality of many not so privileged women.

Your ill-conceived advice missed the one very important point that you should have made. Single mothers need money that could be obtained if the government enforced the court orders for support. Court orders in other types of legal cases are usually taken seriously. Court orders for the support of children are usually ignored. Have you checked on recent statistics on the amount of unpaid child support? This is one of the only types of legal cases where, often, the burden of enforcing a court order falls upon the victim of the crime.

Many, if not most, single mothers conceived their children within a marriage. That point is inconvenient for many Republicans and right-wingers. It creates a conundrum for them. It is more advantageous to blame the victim. Enforcing orders for support could cost votes. Since babies and children don't have power in the voting booth, it is easy to dismiss them.

The failure of the government to respond to this problem has had far reaching, unintended consequences. The most noticeable is the devaluing of marriage. Throughout history one of the most significant benefits of marriage was the protection of children. That is no longer true. Children born within a marriage are not given any preference, nor should they be, when it comes to government enforcement of one of the most basic of all human rights...the right to food and shelter.

Rosemarie Jackowski

A Thank You Note To The President

By: Rosemarie Jackowski / February 10th, 2006

Dear President Chavez,

I am writing today to express my sincere gratitude to you for all that you have done. Your generous contribution of heating oil to homeless shelters and poor households in the United States is appreciated more than you will ever know. Here, in the northern part of our country winter temperatures often fall well below zero. Many citizens have suffered not only discomfort, but also health problems related to the inadequate heating of their homes. Your contribution is being greeted as a miracle. Because of your generosity, I have been passing the word to all of my friends. I have been asking them to buy only Citgo gasoline.

That other president, the one we have in our country, probably has access to more money than you have. Unfortunately, his priorities are not as humanitarian as yours. He has gotten himself, and us too, entangled in a rather gruesome situation in Iraq. Maybe you read about it in your press. It looks like we will be spending all of our money for generations to come on weapons. That brings up another problem. Many in the United States cannot afford health care. If it is not too much trouble, next time you are talking to your friend, Fidel, please tell him we need doctors over here. Also, the need for dentists is so critical that my best friend just relocated from the United States to Costa Rica because she had a toothache.

Well, thank you again. Please say, *"Hello"*, to the wife and family for me. Oh, I almost forgot to say that I admire the people of Venezuela who were smart enough to vote for you. Maybe some of them would be willing to come up here and help us run an election in 2008.

Your friend in Vermont,
Rosemarie Jackowski

••• ——— •••   ••• ——— •••   ••• ——— •••

The New Liberation Movement

By: Rosemarie Jackowski / February 9th, 2006

The recent death of Betty Friedan has once again put the spotlight on the feminist movement. There is no question that during much of history, women have been devalued. There is also no question that Friedan and other leaders of the women's movement are owed a debt of gratitude for their efforts.

But there is another side to this story that is too often dismissed as just unintended consequences. The movement did not always free women and give them more choices. Often, women were forced out of the home to work at jobs even more mundane than the ones they left behind. There was not much liberation afforded to the women who were forced to become bean counters for corporations. Many women were transformed from homemakers into widget makers. Leaving the frying pan behind only to be pushed into the fire was how many viewed the liberation movement.

The movement did not help the black mother in Detroit, or the white mother in Appalachia, or the Hispanic mother in Texas, or the migrant farm family in California. Those on the very bottom of the economic scale were forgotten. In many cases they were left worse off than before. Many were forced out of the home, with no transportation, to travel to a minimum wage job. Mothers were sometimes pressured by the culture and the welfare system to leave their children in unsafe conditions to fend for themselves. A generation of *latch key* children was the result.

In urban centers, many were forced to place their children in less than nurturing day care centers. Mothers left their homes to work at low paying, mind-numbing jobs. Talk to any mother who ever has had to drop her sick child off at a day care center. The myth, that a loving parent could be replaced by even the most dedicated childcare worker, is still creating havoc within the culture. The parent-child relationship has been compromised by this social experiment. A paid employee can never replace a loving mother or father.

It is easy to figure out who benefited the most from the movement. Just follow the money. Many families are on the verge of financial collapse today. Big business and corporations are laughing all the way to the bank. They are the greatest beneficiaries. With the inclusion of so many more women, the work force almost doubled. The pay scale quickly reflected this. In 1950, one worker with a high school diploma could support a family. Now it often takes two wage earners to support a household. Capitalism got a big boost, two workers for the price of one.

One of the consequences of the movement was the trivialization of parenting. Women choosing motherhood over the work place were viewed with suspicion.

It can be argued that there is no higher calling in life than the care and nurturing of others. Noticeably absent from the feminist movement was any support for families, single mothers, mothers in general, or even fathers. Today, more families are opting for home schooling. That is not an option when both parents are employed outside the home.

Some women, who were *papered* with college degrees, did benefit with increased choices in the job market. The history of the movement reflected the culture and values of the upwardly mobile female. Today however, many feminists realize that dedicating one's life to a corporation is less fulfilling than promised.

Title nine, equal pay, and abortion rights have always been at the forefront of the movement. This gives the illusion that all women benefit. The stay-at-home mother has become a second-class citizen. That lifestyle choice should be respected, just as the choice to be childless should be a respected choice.

We need a real women's liberation movement. One that will include all women. One that will give women the choice to stay home and be financially compensated. That is not as impossible as it might seem. One change could make that possible. Simply treat all income within the family as family income. That would eliminate the unfair burden on the stay-at-home parent when

Social Security benefits are calculated. It would also eliminate the harm that comes to children when the wage-earning parent fails to support his/her children. In addition, it would allow more mothers to stay at home and therefore benefit not only children but also all in the workforce. Fewer workers competing for the same number of jobs would increase all wages. It would be a *win-win scenario.*

The new liberation movement must place less emphasis on gender and more emphasis on the common humanity that we all share. Those who need liberation most are those whose voices are not heard...the economically disadvantaged, the homeless, the disabled, and especially the children.

The Deposition

By: Rosemarie Jackowski / January 25th, 2006

> *"A citizen in United States should never expect to gain justice through the judicial system. The system is so corrupted that in the rare case when justice prevails, it is not because of, but it is in spite of, the system."*
> *-R. Jackowski*

For the past several years I have been blessed with a unique learning experience. I have been a defendant and also a plaintiff against the government. My experience as a defendant has received widespread coverage. My conviction in that case is now under appeal in the Vermont Supreme Court and is not the topic of this report. Instead, I am now breaking my long six-year silence about my experience as a plaintiff. There is no connection between the two legal cases.

June 5, 2000 was a beautiful, warm day. It was one of those days that every Vermonter anticipates eagerly after the long, cruel winter. I had just received word that my 89-year-old mother had taken a bad fall in a supermarket parking lot. Her kneecap had been broken. She lived alone, 300 miles distant. She needed my help. I left my house to do last minute errands before departing for Pennsylvania where my mother lived. I drove around the corner from my house and traveled a short distance toward town. Traffic was slow...stop and go.

I was stopped in the line of traffic. Suddenly my small 94 Ford Tempo exploded. It shook violently. The noise was exactly that of an explosion. My body, along with the car, was violently shaking back and forth. I am not sure what happened after that. I remember, after some time, seeing the face of a woman looking in my windshield. Cars were stopped. People had gathered. Police sirens were blaring. I was placed in an ambulance. I then realized that I had been rear-ended by a large dump truck. The truck had additional mass and weight because it was carrying a load of logs. Witness statements all agree that the driver of the truck was looking out the side window at some pretty ladies in shorts. His inattention, speed, and reckless driving were the cause of the accident. The truck was owned and operated by the State of Vermont.

The ride to the hospital in the ambulance was a surreal experience. A police officer was in the emergency room when the ambulance arrived. I was grateful to have another human at my side. As I laid on the gurney, the police officer made a phone call. I heard his side of the conversation in which he said, "*...no, no tickets have been issued...*". When he hung up, I asked him why. I told him, as he could see, I had just been nearly killed. His answer to me was, "*You know how it is. We work together.*" Yes, I understood his sentiment. The old boys' network is a constant topic in small town Bennington.

That should have been a clue to me as to how things would go from then on. It was just the first in a long series of very troubling occurrences. I faced a new crisis each day. Where I live a car is a necessity for survival. There is no public transportation and no municipal water supply. Water must be purchased at the store some distance away, and carried in. One day as I was pleading with the state for a car to replace my car which they had totaled, they offered this solution. The state offered to cut my car in half, find one that had been totaled in the front, and then weld the two pieces together. I rejected that offer and told them that I had just seen an exposé on TV about that type of repair and it was an unsafe and possibly illegal practice.

Being a party to a lawsuit was a totally new experience for me. I had been driving for 50 years, locally and across country. I am a firm believer in defensive driving. It had always worked for me in the past. Being stopped in a line of traffic with no way of escaping a speeding truck approaching from the rear changed my reality. Everyday brought a new challenge. My car was now totaled. I did not have the money to replace it. My life was drastically changed. Howard Dean was governor in 2000. One day in desperation I called his private phone number, which had been given to me by a

     ••• ——— •••   ••• ——— •••   ••• ——— •••

member of the state Legislature. Somehow, I managed to connect with Gov. Dean's personal attorney. I still remember this, because he was one of the few associated with the government who seemed to be polite and compassionate. There was nothing he could do to help.

I began a search for a lawyer. The first one said, *"Rosemarie, this is Vermont. Don't expect any justice here."* Another lawyer said that because of my age, the case would not be profitable enough for him. I soon learned that age discrimination runs rampant through the legal system. Anyone over 50 is at a distinct disadvantage. I was over 60. Money matters.

I was dealing with medical issues as a result of the accident. My finances were destroyed. The hospital put a lien on me because my medical bills had not been paid. My mother was without my help. The only car I had was the one that had been totaled. Life was getting more difficult with each day. Days turned into months...months into years. I now looked at my life in two stages, my life before the accident, and my life after the accident. In the beginning, this was referred to as my life in legal limbo. Now a more accurate description would be my life in legal hell.

Finally, after five years, I was scheduled to be deposed by the state. Oh, I was so ready! I had waited all of these years to talk about the accident. Up until now, because I did not want to embarrass the truck driver who nearly killed me, I had not openly discussed the accident.

The big day arrived. I was taken into a small, windowless room in the state's attorney's office complex. I looked around. There was a one-way mirror opposite to where I was seated. There were some metal bookshelves with black garbage bags on them. It reminded me of Abu Ghraib. I was told to raise my right hand and was sworn in. Then the interrogation by an assistant to the state attorney general began. She asked questions about my political activities… questions about my political writings. She had copied all of them from the Internet and waved them about with great emotion. She seemed excited by the fact that some of my articles had appeared on a web site that has a four-letter word in its name. Obviously, she thought that this would embarrass me. It did not. I calmly explained to her that I do not have a web site and I have no control over what name other people give to their web sites. I don't know if she believed me or not.

Then the interrogation got even more interesting. She asked questions about my sex life. She asked questions about my marriage that had ended 35 years prior. Then she started to ask detailed questions about the fact that I had been the victim of a brutal rape. The rape, which is irrelevant to this case, had occurred 40, yes 40, years ago during a time when I was working in Florida. By now, it had become very clear to me what was happening. There was no doubt in my mind that this was an attempt to intimidate me. I had always believed that witness intimidation was against the law, but what did I know. This was Vermont and I was not a lawyer. The exploitation of any rape victim should never be tolerated. Opening the wounds of a traumatic event such as that would be very painful to most rape victims. I maintained my *"cool"* and took comfort in the fact that it was now obvious what was happening. The strategy of the attorney general's office was now very clear. This was to be a no-holds-barred, fight to the death… a David and Goliath struggle… an attempt to beat me into submission so that I would not seek justice. Would justice prevail, or would this be just one more failed attempt of an injured citizen to gain redress for a wrong?

The morning after the deposition, I picked up a copy of the *Rutland Herald*. It reported a news story about an elderly couple, Edward and Margaret Tateosian, who also had been injured by a state-owned truck. Reading the account of the treatment that they had received from the state was very disturbing. Apparently, their experience was similar to mine. I now was certain that this problem with the state of Vermont was bigger than just one case. How many other victims were out there, I wondered.

During my deposition, and at all other times, I had managed to maintain proper decorum...always remaining polite; however, stress of the accident and its medical and legal aftermath was taking a toll on my health. My intestine started to bleed. After several months, I realized that I could no longer ignore this new stress-related health crisis. At the hospital minor surgery was performed.

On the eve of Christmas Eve, I received the pathology report from the hospital. It described a condition that could eventually be life-threatening. That same day I also received a court order, signed by a judge, demanding that, on January 16, 2006, I travel up north towards the Canadian border to be examined by a doctor who specializes in sports medicine. This was one of the state's expert witnesses. Travel right now was difficult. I had requested permission to see any doctor that the state chose closer to my home. I suggested Albany, N.Y., which is within 50 miles of my residence. There are many doctors in Albany. The court denied my request.

I now was faced with a dilemma. Should I follow the advice of those in the medical community and put my health first, or should I comply with the court order? The fist of the government was coming down in a hard and brutal way. I spent my Christmas holiday trying to figure a way out of this latest legal/medical quagmire.

Meantime I had been researching the topic of *"expert witnesses"*. On the Internet I learned that they are referred to as *"liars for hire"*. This was a whole new growth industry. Of course, the side with the most money to hire the most impressive expert witnesses usually wins the case. Money matters. In legal cases, often it is ONLY money that matters.

January 16, 2006 arrived. It was Martin Luther King Day. I thought about the injustice that he had suffered. I certainly would not compare my problems with the government to his, but every person should be allowed to live with dignity, honor, and justice. I decided to put my health at risk and make the trip up north through the mountains as ordered by the court. The state transported me. It was 3 degrees below zero. A snowstorm had left the roads in a dangerous condition. Cars were off the in the ditches. State police and tow trucks were assisting motorists. I thought about the fact that the state had six June's, six July's, and six August's to impose this trip on me, but instead chose January, the month of the year when the mountain roads are the most dangerous. The trip was 289 miles and took 10 hours. Ten hours without food, except for the water and crackers that I had brought with me.

Because the accident was a rear-ender with many witnesses, this case should have settled in weeks. In my opinion any state is grossly negligent if it places any driver, with a history of accidents, behind the wheel of a truck. This was no accident; it was an accident waiting to happen. It happened to me. It happened to the Teteosians. It has happened to an unknown number of other citizens. It could happen to anyone.

About my mother...without a safe car, I was not able to get to Pennsylvania to give her any assistance. Her health deteriorated. She was placed in a nursing home and she lost the house she had worked a lifetime for. It was taken to pay the cost of the nursing home.

George Bush and others have argued for Tort Reform. I agree that it is needed...in the opposite way than that which has been proposed. In Vermont, the problem is not the bribing of judges. The problem is cronyism and a questionable level of competence. Added to that is a lack of appreciation for fairness and a very troubling lack of humanity.

My past experience as an advocate for children brought me to the courtroom on many occasions. In Vermont I saw jurors sleeping during important testimony. In New Jersey I once saw a judge reading the sports page during crucial testimony.

I offer these suggestions as a start. First, end the culture in the Vermont Attorney General's Office that allows the abuse of citizens, such as that which occurred during my deposition. I hereby publicly offer to teach a consciousness-raising seminar, at no charge, to the Vermont Attorney General and his staff. Second, no case should be allowed to linger and languish in the system for five, six, or seven years. Third, the use of expert witnesses should be totally eliminated or at least minimized. Jurors should always be told when testimony is bought and paid for.

I have written this report as a warning to other citizens. The judicial system is broken. The burden of fixing or replacing the broken system falls upon the people. I have too many suggestions to include all of them here. Any ideas or suggestions from others would be appreciated.

A Small Matter Of Justice

By: Rosemarie Jackowski / December 19th, 2005

There are some good reasons why every U.S. citizen should be thinking about reparations. The payment of reparations to every victim of U.S. foreign and domestic policy would have a dramatic effect on the course of history; but also there are other, often overlooked, advantages that would come from just having a great national debate about reparations. The debate itself would have long lasting rewards. A national conversation about reparations would be the one thing that could awaken and inform the sleeping citizens. This is a nation in which factual information is difficult to come by. School textbooks rarely give an accurate view of history. The combination of a misguided government-owned and operated educational system and an incompetent corporate-owned mass media has resulted in a misinformed, sleeping populace.

Reparations could change everything. Many citizens think with their wallets. If every citizen had to think about having a huge increase in taxes to pay for past actions taken by the government, it could result in a demand for change in U.S. policies. A war tax would make war less likely. A reparations tax would make the exploitation of others around the globe less likely.

Any debate about reparations would take the discussion back to the time of Columbus. Why should those living now feel a sense of responsibility for events that occurred at a time so far in the past? The answer is because those events from the distant past are having negative effects on the lives of so many Native Americans now. That same answer can be used to justify reparations to our black brothers and sisters. The destruction of the culture of the original inhabitants of the land which we now occupy has had a profound affect on Native Americans here today. The same can be said about the destruction of the family life and culture of those who were victimized by the slave trade.

Right now there are groups of victims who are seeking justice. The Vietnam victims of Agent Orange are seeking a legal remedy. On March 10, 2005, in District Court in Brooklyn, Judge Jack Weinstein dismissed the case. Will the U.S. ever do the right thing and compensate the Vietnam victims? Certainly not, unless there is a debate that will awaken the sleeping American conscience. Today, high levels of dioxin are found in the soil, food, human blood, and breast milk of the Vietnam victims. The Vietnam victims should no longer be subjected to a torturous legal battle. The Congress should pass legislation that would compensate them. Reparations must be paid now.

Currently, in a British court, other victims of U.S. policy are pleading their case. The Chagossians, who inhabited Diego Garcia until they were forcibly removed by the U.S., have been waging an ongoing legal battle. Currently that case is in adjournment until January 19, 2006. These inhabitants were forcibly loaded on boats and shipped off. They were removed from their peaceful island homeland after the U.S. incinerated their pets and animals. The displaced people have petitioned for the right to visit the graves of their ancestors on Diego Garcia. Their petition has been denied. The U.S. policy that led to this ethnic cleansing/genocide is still in place. The Pentagon wanted this island as a location for a military base which has been used as the launching pad for the bombing campaign against Iraq. The U.S. base should be decommissioned. The land should be decontaminated. The people should be allowed to return to their homeland. Reparations should be paid.

The list of countries that have a legitimate claim against the U.S. is staggering...Mexico, Cuba, Vietnam, Grenada, Nicaragua, Panama, Iran, Libya, Afghanistan, Iraq, just to name a few. Fair compensation would certainly deplete the national treasury for generations to come. That is the price that must be paid so that victimized nations all around the world might be a little safer from future invasions and occupations.

Reparations must be paid not only to compensate victims, but also to rehabilitate our fallen nation so that future generations can chart a new course. Restitution is a universally accepted legal and moral principle. Put simply, those who kill, should pay the bill. No amount of money can compensate for even one lost life. That is precisely why this national conversation is necessary. News reports often mention the financial cost of military operations in Iraq to taxpayers, but there is rarely a mention of the cost in human lives to the victims in Iraq. Every citizen should see the photos of babies born to mothers who had been exposed to U.S. depleted uranium. The decontamination and rebuilding of Iraq should be managed by the Iraqi people and totally financed by U.S. taxpayers.

There is no better way to challenge U.S. foreign policies that have resulted in death and exploitation around the globe than to tell taxpayers that they will have to pay for it. A war tax is necessary because it would make wars much less likely. A reparations tax is necessary because it is the best way of informing everyone of past transgressions. Besides that, it is the only way to redemption for a country that is in need of an awakened conscience....and yes, there is also a small matter of justice.

From Hiroshima To Fallujah: The Slaughter Of Civilians Continues

By: Rosemarie Jackowski / July 18th, 2005

Below is the TOP SECRET, now declassified, document that ordered the first use of the atomic bomb.

25 July 1945

TO: General Carl Spaatz Commanding General United States Army Strategic Air Forces

1. The 509 Composite Group, 20th Air Force will deliver its first special bomb as soon as weather will permit visual bombing after about 3 August 1945 on one of the targets: Hiroshima, Kokura, Niigata and Nagasaki. To carry military and civilian scientific personnel from the War Department to observe and record the effects of the explosion of the bomb, additional aircraft will accompany the airplane carrying the bomb. The observing planes will stay several miles distant from the point of impact of the bomb.

2. Additional bombs will be delivered on the above targets as soon as made ready by the project staff. Further instructions will be issued concerning targets other than those listed above.

3. Discussion of any and all information concerning the use of the weapon against Japan is reserved to the Secretary of War and the President of the United States. No communiques on the subject or releases of information will be issued by Commanders in the field without specific prior authority. Any news stories will be sent to the War Department for specific clearance.

••• ――― •••   ••• ――― •••   ••• ――― •••

It is important to note that this document does not order any protection for the civilian population. It does not specify that only military sites be targeted. The U.S. rules of engagement now are basically the same as they were 60 years ago, on August 6, 1945.

The targeting of cities, which are large population centers, continues today. The pattern of slaughtering civilians remains unchanged. Victims of U.S. bombing campaigns during the last 60 years include civilians in China, Guatemala, Indonesia, Cuba, Congo, Peru, Laos, Vietnam, Cambodia, Grenada, Libya, El Salvador, Nicaragua, Panama, Iraq, Sudan, Afghanistan, and Yugoslavia. *Lancet* estimates that more than 100,000 civilian deaths have resulted from the U.S. military campaign in Iraq. Now, as the war and occupation continue, the deaths of civilians continue.

No nation that has a history of such irresponsible use of any weapon system should remain unchallenged. The citizens of the U.S. must bring their government into compliance with International Law. Provisions of the Geneva Convention clearly prohibit the targeting of civilian populations. The use of WMD's against civilians is not an accident. History shows that it has been a deliberate, planned, consistent U.S. policy for more than 60 years. Cluster bombs, land mines, and the fire bombing strategy of shock-and-awe type campaigns are designed to terrorize the civilian population. The U.S. bombing of Iraq has occurred on a regular basis since 1991.

The deaths caused by the illegal, genocidal blockade of Iraq far outnumber the deaths at Hiroshima and Nagasaki. This is not meant to trivialize the deaths in Japan, but rather to show that the policy of using civilian deaths as a strategy of war continues to this day.

In May of 1996, on 60 Minutes, UN Ambassador Madeleine Albright stated that the deaths of a half million Iraqi children was *"worth it"*. The Ambassador's statement has been heard around the world and, in part, explains why they hate us. Is there a U.S. citizen anywhere who would not be offended if someone from another country said that a half million of our children should be sacrificed for their political/economic agenda?

Perhaps the best way to honor the victims of Hiroshima and Nagasaki would be to challenge the U.S. policy, as stated by Albright, that the deaths of children are *"worth it."*

Here Comes The Judge, And He's Coming For Your House

By: Rosemarie Jackowski / June 24th, 2005

> *"..Any property may now be taken for the benefit of another private party, but the fallout from this decision will not be random. The beneficiaries are likely to be those citizens with disproportionate influence and power in the political process, including large corporations and development firms..."*
> -Justice Sandra Day O'Connor, writing in dissent

So you worked all of your life and all that you have to show for it is a little place on Elm Street. It's not much, but it is home. It's your castle. It's where you built a lifetime of memories, raised your children, held family gatherings, had friends over for dinner. Well guess what. You better start packing because at any moment there may be a knock on the door. A man will be there saying that he is from the government and he is there to help you. He is there to help you give up your little castle. It is almost as if life in the good ol' U.S. of A. has become a bad joke.

This whole Eminent Domain issue seems like a nightmare at the moment, but maybe there is a silver lining in this dark cloud. This is one issue where the Left and the Right agree. The combined efforts from all spectrums of the political landscape might be enough to turn this boondoggle for the elite around.

We better not get too optimistic though. This Eminent Domain issue is just one problem. Another issue that leaves every citizen vulnerable is the issue of Sovereign Immunity. Talk to anyone who has ever been injured by a government owned vehicle. If Eminent Domain doesn't get you, Sovereign Immunity will.

They Had A Coup d'etat And We Weren't Invited ... Now It's Our Turn

By: Rosemarie Jackowski / June 19th, 2005

Exactly when was it that the citizens of the United States lost their country? When did the coup take place and how did I miss it? Maybe I was rotating my tires that night.

There is plenty of evidence that somewhere along the line, we all have lost any influence that we might have had as citizens. Think about the Downing Street Memo. That should be enough to convince even the most ardent fan of the Republican or Democratic Party. That memo is just an echo of the Project for a New American Century.

Amnesty International has recently released a report about the Archipelago of U.S. gulags. Several years ago, I contacted all three of my men in Washington. I requested information about the number and locations of U.S. prisons in foreign countries. I also wanted to know how many prisoners were being held at each location and what their countries of origin were.

Surely our members of Congress would have that information. Wrong. My Washington delegation is usually prompt at honoring requests, but this time all three failed to come forth with any information. Yes, I know about FOIA. I remember thinking at the time, if the members of Congress don't know what is going on, who is running the show in Washington?

Did we lose our country during the reign of Ollie North? No, I don't think so. I vaguely remember him being interviewed back then. As I remember, he explained that he and the others in the cabal had a plan for a coup but never actually pulled it off because it was not necessary. The coup had already taken place.

Did the coup happen way back on July 26, 1947 when President Truman signed the National Security Act, which authorized a Black Budget? Maybe, I am not sure. What I do know for sure is that until we eliminate the Black Budget, we should not pretend that we have a democracy. If you can't follow the money, you cannot be an informed citizen. If the National Security Act of 1947 authorizes the withholding of important information from the voters, it follows that informed consent has been lacking at the polls; therefore, every national election since 1947 should be declared invalid. The authorization of a Black Budget not only allows government deception; it encourages and rewards it. Also there is the little matter of a conflict with the U.S. Constitution...specifically Article 1, Section 9. It states "*...a regular Statement and Account of the Receipts and Expenditures of all public money shall be published...*"

So when did the coup happen and why were we not invited? I feel deprived...kind of like not being invited to your own family's family reunion. Think of the dark, smoke filled rooms, the Jim Beam and Chivas Regal flowing like water, all paid for by us and we were not invited. Think of all of those white guys in suits and probably some of them in uniforms, drinking our booze and eating our hor d'oeuvres...the laughter, the jokes, the pseudo-intellectual conversation...kind of like a cocktail party for killers, hell-bent on building empires for themselves. They had all of the fun and all that we got was the bill and to top it off, we lost our country in the process.

It's just not fair. They got to play at Empire Building while we worked in the factories and schools and hospitals. They had fun while we worked. It is time to even the score. Now it's our turn. What we need is a coup to undo their coup. How can we make that happen? Many of my friends are dedicated to the non-violence movement, out of respect for them, I would consider a non-violent action. Sort of a *rumble without the tumble.* I don't see much chance for success with that strategy, so I challenge anyone out there to come up with a winning idea that would be effective.

We respect the Rule of Law and that puts us at a big disadvantage as compared to those in power. We follow the rules and they don't. The playing field is not equal. They have money and bombs

   ••• ––– •••   ••• ––– •••   ••• ––– •••

and an army and two political parties and all that we have is proof that they have been lying to us for a very long time. I don't see a light at the end of this very dark tunnel but there is a remote possibility that we can turn things around. The call for impeachment is gaining momentum. The timing is perfect right now and timing is everything. If we all join the Impeachment Movement, maybe we can finally win one battle in what will be a very long war, a war to take back our country.

George Bush needs to be Impeached not because he is responsible for the current state of affairs but because Impeachment will show those who are behind him with the real power, that the people are rising up. When the people rise up, they will demand justice for the slaughtered victims of many overt and covert military actions. War crimes trials of the Washington war criminals will be sure to follow. This is not exactly an impossible dream. Consider this, the majority of people around the world are waiting for us to get our government under control. Many are eager to help because they feel the threat that comes from a global empire. This militaristic global empire, with a history of using nuclear weapons, is feared and hated by many around the world.

Also, we must end the Black Budget, once and for all. He who controls the Black Budget controls everything. No democracy can exist alongside of a secret shadow government. The U.S. Constitution must either be followed or amended. The time has come to end the Constitutional crisis that has been created by this secret unauthorized branch of government. We must call for federal legislation that will make any Black Budget, now or in the future, illegal. Support of the Black Budget is an act of treason and should be prosecuted as such. Currently in Washington there is no one with the courage necessary to frame legislation that would end this secret stream of money that finances the killing and oppression of people all over the globe. The burden of eliminating the Black Budget will fall upon the citizens in this country and around the world.

The Impeachment of George Bush and the elimination of the Black Budget would not solve all of our problems, but they would be big steps in the right direction.

••• ——— •••   ••• ——— •••   ••• ——— •••

Informing The Citizenry: Churchill And The Newscaster

By: Rosemarie Jackowski / February 8th, 2005

Thank you, Ward Churchill...for doing the impossible and opening up a national discussion about U.S. foreign policy.

Ward Churchill's controversial essay has served a very important purpose for which the world should be eternally grateful. It has opened a national discussion about responsibility, guilt, and foreign policy. This discussion is long overdue. It is not about how many angels can dance on the head of a pin. It is about how many citizens must accept responsibility for the actions taken by their government in their names. Churchill's essay is an essay about you and me.

Though guilt is often used as a religious term, the connection to religion is not a necessary one. An atheist might have an even greater appreciation for ethical or moral behavior than a religious person because the atheist would not hold the belief, common to most religions, that the afterlife would be the time for ultimate justice. Maybe an atheist would be more apt to work for justice in this life.

Guilt is an essential part of the human psyche. It is the voice of the conscience. It is the force that can turn a battlefield soldier into a conscientious objector. Ward Churchill, in his essay, was trying to awaken the conscience in each of us. Maybe he was trying to teach us that humanity will continue to suffer until we all become conscientious objectors. He was echoing the message of Gandhi, Martin Luther King, Malcolm X, and many other peace and justice advocates of the past.

Churchill makes reference to workers in some career fields, which can be associated with the harm done by the government. He refers to them as *"technocrats of the empire"*. Can that be interpreted to include, among others, those working in the financial field? Without financial support, the war machine could not function. Not

   ••• — — — •••   ••• — — — •••   ••• — — — •••

too long ago, a family in Massachusetts, as a matter of conscience, refused to pay their taxes. The family was prepared to pay a high price for their heroic act of conscience. The government confiscated the family's home.

Assigning levels of guilt or responsibility would be an interesting topic for debate. Does the financier bear a greater burden of guilt than the technician? What about the person who pays his taxes knowing that some portion will go to support the war? What about the educator who fails to give his students an accurate worldview? What about the scientist in the weapons laboratory? What about the professor who taught the scientist in the laboratory? What about the auto mechanic who repaired the car of the professor, and thus enabled the professor to get to work?

Does the pilot who flies the plane have the same level of guilt as the bombardier who releases the cluster bombs? What about the factory worker who made the sprocket that went into the plane? What about the technician in the micro-technology lab? How about the bystander at a parade, who cheers on the war machine? What about the commander-in-chief? What about the low ranking soldier on the battlefield? Does the military chaplain who gives aid and comfort to a soldier, during an illegal war, carry a burden of guilt? There are varying degrees of responsibility. Maybe history will exonerate none of us.

Religious and legal experts generally agree that knowledge and understanding are necessary in order to hold a person responsible. Would a commander-in-chief be morally responsible for his deadly policies if he lacked the information necessary to make an informed decision? The lack of information might give a president an escape clause in the social/moral contract. Because of that, there is one group that has an even higher level of moral responsibility...one group that must accept the guilt for the millions slaughtered in deserts, jungles, and bombed out cities. The Ultimate Guilt falls upon those who control the dissemination of information...those who control the Press and the electronic media.

••• ——— •••   ••• ——— •••   ••• ——— •••

Maybe at a time of extreme crisis, when civilians are being bombed there should be a moratorium on all coverage of hyped up sex trials of celebrities, sporting events, and other irrelevant shows of questionable news value. Can it be justified to have a Super Bowl during a super humanitarian crisis? Pleasure, joy, fun, and celebration are important aspects of the human experience, but our national priorities should be examined. If we have 20 TV sports channels and not one foreign policy channel, one might come to the conclusion that our national focus is a bit twisted.

Judging by the number of people who still believe the big WMD lie, the news/talk shows that are aired have failed to inform. Part of the problem is that the members of the media do not know what they don't know. Would the fact that they also are uninformed relieve them of any responsibility? Maybe, but maybe not. Certainly the members of the Press have a responsibility to at least make a minimal effort to gain information. They have not been doing that. They have failed in their sacred trust.

We need a pledge in the spirit of the Hippocratic Oath for those who broadcast the news. Would they be willing to, at least, *do no harm*? If they are not inspired enough to educate and inform themselves, they should turn their microphones and presses over to someone who cares enough to access the relevant information, especially on topics of life and death, war and peace.

The list of topics that have been ignored by the press, resulting in the deaths of innocent civilians, is a long one. One of the many neglected news stories that needs to be explored is the government policy as expressed by Madeleine Albright on May 12, 1996. In an answer to Leslie Stahl on 60 Minutes, Albright stated that the deaths of 500,000 Iraqi children were *"worth it"*. Albright was not just a person in the checkout line in the supermarket. Albright was speaking as an official of the government. The *"it was worth it"* statement has been hanging out there in the airways for almost nine years. The world has been waiting for years for a member of the press to investigate that policy of the government of the United States. Please, ask the question at the next press conference. The question is, *"Does United States official policy still support the idea*

  ••• ――― •••   ••• ――― •••   ••• ――― •••

that the deaths of large numbers of children can be justified, in order to promote U.S. foreign policy?"

There are those who accuse Churchill of being an extremist. Instead, it seems that his views are really quite moderate. There are others who are calling for a complete shutdown of the economy, the closing of all businesses, and a boycott of all, except essential services, as long as the wars and occupations continue.

I thank Ward Churchill for opening the discussion with his essay. At a time in history when one nation has a stash of weapons of mass destruction sufficient to kill every living thing on the planet, no one has a greater responsibility than the newscaster. It is only an informed citizenry which holds any hope for the survival of humanity. Maybe someday, if the Press fulfills its moral mandate, there will be no more 9/11s.

Super Patriot, Ward Churchill

By: Rosemarie Jackowski / February 2nd, 2005

From Scarborough Country to the Spin Zone, the attacks on Professor Ward Churchill are coming across the airwaves. Near Hamilton College in Clinton, New York the hills are alive with the sound of fascism.

In a statement released on January 31, 2005, Churchill says, *"...The bottom line of my argument is that the best and perhaps only way to prevent 9-1-1-style attacks on the U.S. is for American citizens to compel their government to comply with the rule of law. The lesson of Nuremberg is that this is not only our right, but our obligation. To the extent we shirk this responsibility, we, like the "Good Germans" of the 1930s and '40s, are complicit in its actions and have no legitimate basis for complaint when we suffer the consequences. This, of course, includes me, personally, as well as my family, no less than anyone else..."*

Please notice that Churchill does not exclude himself and his family from responsibility. The argument that all of us share in the guilt for the actions of our government is seldom accepted, yet can not be ultimately denied. For centuries, the most respected scholars have postulated that any government derived from the will of the populace requires the active and willing participation of its citizens. When the bloated, nihilistic, self-absorbed populace denies its responsibility for the firm entrenchment of a defacto royal family, known as the Bush dynasty, our commitment to the basic tenets of the U.S. Constitution, and humanity everywhere, is poorly served. But let's not be too harsh on the Bush dynasty. Much has happened under the Clinton and other administrations. Churchill explains that it is the actions of the U.S. that brought about 9/11. That is such an obvious and simple fact that it is remarkable that there is anyone left who still doesn't get it. It is simple and obvious. It is not rocket science. It is Blowback. *Blowback* is a term coined by the CIA many years ago because those in the CIA knew that U.S. policies would result in blowback.

Anyone who did not know that there would be some retaliation against the U.S. was not paying attention.

Remember May 12, 1996, when Madeleine Albright was asked on 60 Minutes about the deaths of 500,000 Iraqi children. Her answer was, *"...we think the price is worth it."* That should be the focus of the national discussion. Were those 500,000 deaths plus the deaths of the additional 100,000 slaughtered Iraqi civilians worth the price that we may eventually have to pay? Until that national discussion takes place, we are a nation in denial, a dysfunctional nation divorced from reality. Those who control the major means of communication do not have the right to prevent that discussion. The time has come for us, the people, to take control of the airways, which we already own.

There should have been a great national debate before the Gulf War. U.S. Ambassador April Glaspie gave Saddam the go ahead for his invasion into Kuwait and then the U.S. used that as an excuse for the Gulf War. That was a case of bait and switch, which resulted in the slaughter of thousands. Then came the deaths of the 500,000 Iraqi children and the official statement that *it was worth it.*

I propose a series of great national debates. On one side there could be experts such as William Blum, Ward Churchill, John Perkins, Ralph Nader, Mickey Z., Howard Zinn, Noam Chomsky, and/or Gore Vidal. There are too many who are well informed to list them all here. The opposing side would pick experts. The debate question is, *Were the deaths of the 500,000 children worth it, or should there be a change in U.S. Foreign Policy.* Let the debate begin.

The members of the uninformed Press would have us believe that the attack on the Twin Towers was just a coincidence... that there was no logical reason why those two buildings were selected out of the millions of tall buildings that exist on the planet. Unfortunately, the uninformed behind the microphones, don't know what they do not know. Yet they continue to mold public opinion. The news broadcasters don't have a sufficient understanding of the effects of U.S. foreign policy, to enter in to a discussion. They have to resort to ad hominem attacks on Ward Churchill and anyone else who questions or criticizes the government.

Meantime the doomsday clock is ticking away and other attacks, similar to 9/11, are predicted unless we learn the lessons that Churchill is teaching. He says, "*...the best and perhaps only way to prevent 9-1-1-style attacks on the U.S. is for American citizens to compel their government to comply with the rule of law.*" Churchill is trying to protect his fellow citizens. He is a humanitarian, a super patriot, and a gifted scholar. We would all be much safer if he was appointed National Director of Homeland Security or, better yet, Secretary of State. Come to think of it, I like the sound of President Ward Churchill.

Iraqi Order 81...Orders, Occupation, And Oppression

By; Rosemarie Jackowski / February 1st, 2005

How did this happen? While few of us were paying attention, the Coalition Provisional Authority, representing the government of the United States, imposed a set of 100 orders on Iraq. A careful examination of these orders could lead to the conclusion that the war is being waged to enrich corporations at the expense of the ordinary citizens. Many of these orders take freedom and liberty away from the people of Iraq. The orders also have a profound effect on us.

Iraqi Order 81 is of special interest because it goes a long way in affecting every living being on the planet. This order prohibits Iraqi farmers from using the methods of agriculture that they have used for centuries. The common worldwide practice of saving heirloom seeds from one year to the next is now illegal in Iraq. Order 81 wages war on Iraqi farmers. They have lost the freedom and liberty to choose their own methods of agriculture.

The food chain has been under worldwide assault by U.S. corporations for some time now. The Master Race of corporations has seized control of the very essence of life itself. We are now in the age of Genetically Modified Doomsday Seeds.

This is not exactly a new phenomenon. It has been a gradual takeover. Remember Percy Schmeiser, the Canadian farmer, who was sued by Monsanto? Not enough people stood up for Percey, so then *they* came for other farmers. In fact, Monsanto has sued so many farmers that a national hotline (1-888-FARMHLP) has now been set up to assist them.

Those who have been pushing for Tort Reform never mention the frivolous, mean-spirited lawsuits brought by Monsanto against U.S. farmers. This is a David and Goliath battle and, as usual, our government is on the side of Goliath. Order 81 now spreads the assault on farmers to Iraq. The domino effect is underway. The victim farmers in the U.S., Iraq, Canada, and all of the other countries who have been under attack by Monsanto need our help. The Tort Reform that is really needed would be reform aimed at compensating victims of corporate intimidation.

The corporations, backed up by the Pentagon, have been jack-booting and goose stepping their way across the planet. Whether you like it or not, you probably will have some franken food on your dinner plate tonight… franken foods, grown from franken seeds, brought to you compliments of the Franken Empire. Our own USDA was complicit in the development of Terminator seeds. Picture Dr. Strangelove on the John Deere.

The existence of Order 81, and the other 99 orders, which limit Iraqi liberty and freedom, creates some interesting questions. How can Washington even pretend that the election in Iraq is legitimate if U.S. imposed rules are enforced after the election, or are we to believe that the 100 Orders are canceled by the election? I don't think so.

Is it possible that Iraqi farmers think back fondly to the good old days before the Occupation and before Order 81? Even Saddam Hussein allowed them to save seeds for the next year's crop. Is Monsanto a worse master than Saddam? Imagine what would happen if there was a successful worldwide movement of resistance, an international *Save the Seed Campaign*. Farmers and consumers in the U.S. need to stand in solidarity with the farmers and consumers in Iraq.

If you have a stamp or coin collection, forget it. Instead, it might be better to start collecting seeds. Maybe soon, one good old-fashioned seed that was made by Mother Nature will be more precious than your most prized gold coin. Just one more thing… if you save seeds, keep it a secret. The Seed Police have been on patrol. They are looking for you.

On Town Meeting Day, 2004, in Vermont, the citizens in seventy-nine towns passed resolutions against genetically engineered crops.

Then Vermont made history when it became the first state to require the labeling of Genetically Modified seeds. *"The Farmer Protection Act is a pre-emptive strike to stop predatory lawsuits against Vermont's family farmers by biotech companies like Monsanto,"* said Ben Davis with the Vermont Public Interest Research Group. Maybe this small, but hard-fought, victory gives reason to hope for a better world.

A Conversation With A Hit Man - Welcome To Loan Shark Nation

By: Rosemarie Jackowski / January 19th, 2005

John Perkins' new book, *Confessions of an Economic Hit Man*, is a must read, even for the well informed who already have an understanding of the dark side of Capitalism. The book paints a mental picture of the hows and whys, the nuts and bolts, of how the Empire exploits and enslaves people around the world under the guise of helping them. John Perkins gives new meaning to the statement, *I'm from the government, and I am here to help you. Now the entire world is put on notice to be on guard when anyone says, I'm from the World Bank, or the IMF, or the consulting firm, or the engineering company and I am here to help you.*

Rosemarie Jackowski: *Hi, John. First I would like to congratulate you, not only on the completion and success of your book, but the even greater achievement...the changing of the course of your life. The struggle and crisis of conscience that brought you to the point where you are today, I am sure was painful. It appears that you have overcome the many temptations and offers of reward that would have come to you if you had continued your work as a hit man for the empire. I read the book in three sittings. It was absorbing, depressing, and inspiring, all at the same time. I understand that you had been thinking about writing the book for about 20 years but did not do it because of threats and bribes. Have you had any unpleasant occurrences since the book was published? Have there been any offers to make a film based on the book? Somehow, the information in your book has to get into the mainstream.*

John Perkins: As described in the Preface, one publisher took me out to dinner in NYC to tell me that it was a book that needed to be published but he could not publish it without fear of losing his job. After that over a dozen of the world's biggest publishers followed suit. Now that it is out, it is making lots of waves—#1 on Amazon its first week in publication, and has been on *NY Times* bestseller list for a month.

   ••• ––– •••   ••• ––– •••   ••• ––– •••

RJ: When I first heard about your book, it brought to mind the ideas of Gen. Smedley Butler. I know that others have also made that comparison to "Confessions of an Economic Hit Man". After I started reading the book, it brought to mind things that happened in the mid-west to the farmers there in the 1970's. I interviewed some of them at the time, and they described similar fraudulent practices that resulted in the loss of their farms...on perhaps a much smaller scale than the international saga that you describe. Do you have an opinion about that problem?

JP: No personal experience with those farmers. I don't like to speculate, just talk about things I know about from my own experiences.

RJ: Could you name the top 5 or 6 companies which are presently involved in the kind of fraudulent exploitation that you describe?

JP: Of course we all hear about Bechtel and Halliburton. In addition, name any company that does lots of international work and/or uses World Bank money to build large projects, and you've got it. In the Preface I mention Monsanto, GE, Nike, GM, Wal-Mart—good for starters, but the list is long. Of the 100 biggest world economies today, 52 are corporations, not governments. They all participate in this.

RJ: Can you name anyone in Washington who has an enlightened view and who would be helpful in ending this system of exploitation?

JP: I believe change in a democracy must come from the grass roots. When we the people demand a government for, by, and of the people—rather than for, by, and of the corporations, the right politicians will step forward.

RJ: Is there anything important that you left out of the book that you can talk about now?

JP: Lots. It will be in the next book.

RJ: I really look forward to your next book! Within the past few days there was a news report that Argentina had considered simply not paying its debt to the World Bank. It seems to me, that that is the best way to fix the problem. What would be the downside, if the debtor nations just refused to pay?

JP: You asked the trillion dollar question! During recent elections, six Lat Am nations have voted in candidates opposed to U.S. and/or corp globalization: Argentina, Brazil, Chile, Ecuador, Uruguay, and Venezuela. Many countries are discussing not paying their debts—in fact saying it is not really their debt at all but rather debt imposed on them by the corporatocracy and a few corrupt politicians in their countries who were our puppets. What if they all refused to pay? It is a big *"What if"* and not likely to happen given the current economic realities and of how most of the world views our power and our ruthlessness. What if journalists like you were able to convince the American public that we should demand debt forgiveness?

RJ: Ah, that is one of my greatest dreams. We have to get the word out to the debtor nations that they will be doing a service to humanity if they refuse to pay. That is the way to protect those in the future from such exploitation. Your book ends on an upbeat note. You say on page 222, "...Imagine if the Nike swoosh, MacDonald's arches, and Coca-Cola logo became symbols of companies whose primary goals were to clothe and feed the world's poor...". I am not as optimistic as you are.

JP: How can you NOT be optimistic? 90 years ago women could not vote in the U.S. 50 years ago blacks could not ride on the same buses as whites in many parts of this country. Nelson Mandela was in prison for nearly 3 decades and then became pres of S Af and got rid of Apartheid. The U.S. spent $ billions to overthrow the USSR and in the end it was a change of consciousness—led by a small group of labor leaders, playwrights, and poets—that brought the Soviet Union down, and on and on. Do you not think George Washington and all the signers of the Declaration did not face as a great an adversary as you and I today—the mightiest empire in the history of the world at the time? They stuck their heads in nooses— every one would have been hanged as a traitor and terrorist had we lost the Revolution. Pessimism is self-defeating and flies in the face of history. It is pure cowardice. We need courage today.

RJ: I believe that part of the problem is inherent in the Capitalistic System. Under the Predatory Capitalistic system, as it is practiced now in the United States, everything is contaminated by greed...the culture, the economy, the workplace, the educational institutions, and both foreign and domestic policy. It appears that the Court System would not be helpful in righting the wrongs that have been done. The fundamental aspects of our culture play a big role in furthering the evils of Empire. I think about what we teach our children, both in and out of schools. Thank you for calling for a

   ••• ––– •••   ••• ––– •••   ••• ––– •••

revolution in our approach to education. Can you give any specifics about how you would change education? Also, please comment on the shocking failure of our Business Schools and Engineering Schools when it comes to teaching business ethics. Has the ability of our colleges and universities, to teach an accurate global view, been compromised because of government grants and government financed research projects?

JP: Yes. Let's insist on something better.

RJ: I apologize for being so pessimistic. I have been very troubled by the recent actions of our government, especially the killing of so many civilians in Iraq. Every day I look at the photos of the children who were killed with U.S. cluster bombs. On the brighter side, your book has inspired me to come up with a plan of action. On the top of my list would be to encourage debtor nations to announce that they will NOT pay back the loans. Many loans were given in an obvious attempt to defraud and exploit. Second, we must call for reparations to the people who have been enslaved and exploited. Third, we must get the word out. Your book has done a great job of that, but we live in a country that is so morally bankrupt, and so lacking in compassion, that it does not even care about the more than 100,000 civilians we have just slaughtered, so I am not hopeful. I think that part of the answer is to get the information out in other countries, where people seem to be more open minded. In what other countries has your book been published?

JP: Rights already sold in Germany, Brazil, Japan, Korea, being negotiated in many other countries.

RJ: Is there anything else that you would like to add here before we close?

JP: I understand your pessimism. but please know that these are exactly the times that call for hope and action. My experience is that people in many other countries already know that we give them $ billions and that only their rich families and our corps benefit while their lives just get worse. Telling them is telling people who already are aware and essentially powerless. What can a peasant farmer or slum dweller do against us? It is we who must foment the change. It is our people you must reach and inspire. Only action on our part will create the kinds of change we need. We have more resources than any country in history and now we must use them to spread the dream of our founding fathers of life, liberty and the pursuit of happiness for all people around the planet.

RJ: *Thank you. Please stay in touch.*

JP: My pleasure. Please keep up your good work. We must remain diligent and skeptical, and yet at the same time listen to the lessons of history—we can change things. Remember that within *"Emergence"* there is *"Emerge"*. . .

   ••• — — — •••   ••• — — — •••   ••• — — — •••

Shameful Harvest: An American Tradition

By: Rosemarie Jackowski / January 8th, 2005

> *"We hold these truths to be self-evident, that all men are created equal, that they are endowed by their Creator with certain unalienable Rights, that among these are Life, Liberty and the pursuit of Happiness."*
> —Thomas Jefferson

> *"Give me your tired, your poor, Your huddled masses yearning to breathe free, The wretched refuse of your teeming shore. Send these, the homeless, tempest-tost to me, I lift my lamp beside the golden door!"*
> —Emma Lazarus

The Declaration of Independence has been shredded and Lady Liberty has been shunned. The United States does not practice the ideals that those icons represent. We should stop the hypocrisy. The wide support of Arizona Prop. 200 is a perfect example of how low our humanity has fallen.

The U.S.-Mexican border should be completely open. There is no logical reason for restricting travel back and forth across that border.

The threat of terrorism is serious and is a direct result of U.S. foreign policy; but does anyone really believe that, even if every linear inch of our southern border was patrolled, we would be safer? A threat to safety is less likely to originate at our southern border than many other places. The entire eastern seaboard is far more vulnerable, with its thousands of hidden coves, fishing camps, and the hundreds of miles of the intercoastal waterway. Of course, concern about terrorism is not the real reason for the attention being given to the border. The real reason is racism and economic classism. Also, there is the myth that *"they"* are draining our resources. In fact, the opposite is true. Many undocumented workers contribute to the Social Security system and never collect from it.

Our brothers and sisters from south of the border should not only be welcomed but should be welcomed with open arms. They have worked for generations in our Harvests of Shame. In 1960, CBS Reports aired the documentary, *Harvest of Shame*. This is still one of the best films ever produced. It showed the extreme abuse suffered by farm workers and migrant laborers in the U.S. An excellent updated version aired on PBS Frontline, *New Harvest, Old Shame*. Hopefully, those who support Arizona Prop. 200 will educate themselves and re-think their positions.

For generations, the United States has been benefiting from the backbreaking labor of those who work the fields. We must start paying our debt to farm workers. Farm workers comprise the most necessary and the most under appreciated work force in our nation. Their work is sometimes life threatening and almost always hazardous, due to exposure to the chemicals introduced into our food supply by large farming operations. Housing conditions are usually sub-standard.

The Southwest is not the only location of cheap, imported, farm labor. In the Northeast, some of the apple crop is harvested by workers from the Caribbean Islands. They work hard, support the local economy, and they should be offered a full package of benefits, including health coverage, educational opportunities, and pension plans. The apple pickers usually do not bring their families with them, so the U.S. should build and finance hospitals and schools in the islands for the families left in the Caribbean. The workers should also be given the option of relocating with their families to the U.S.

Remember the image of President Reagan sternly demanding, *"Tear down that wall..."* ? We are such masters of hypocrisy. We need a loud national voice that will demand, *"Open that border."* To do less than that, is a public admission of the depths to which our national conscience has fallen.

If all men are created equal, then it follows that all men are deserving of the same dignity, respect, and legal rights. The denial of equal legal rights to anyone, because of the location of his birth, places an unfair burden, a kind of *Birth Tax*, on him. To grant anyone privilege based on the geographical location of his mother, at the time of his birth, is a violation of the fundamental principles of democracy.

Why Panama - Peace On Earth, Good Will Toward Men... American Style

By: Rosemarie Jackowski / December 19th, 2004

It was a quiet and gentle night
Filled with joy and childhood's delight
Some families recited a solemn prayer
While seasonal music filled the night air
Anticipation filled every girl and boy
Who eagerly awaited a holiday toy
It was a time for celebrating Peace on Earth
A time to honor every child's birth

Meanwhile, in Washington plans were underway
For a holocaust on that very day
The year was 1989, the twentieth of December
A day of infamy, that the world will always remember

Suddenly the silent night air was pierced with a strange vibration
But still the children played with eager anticipation
The strange vibration grew louder, just like approaching thunder
Could it be an airplane, one could only listen and wonder
Suddenly explosions were everywhere
It looked as if bombs were bursting in air
To the sleepy village that was preparing for Santa Claus
The President had sent Operation Just Cause

All hope and joy gave way to fright
Fear and horror filled this historic night
A demonic order from the Commander-in-chief
Brought death and destruction and endless grief
Planes dropping death right out of the sky
Left a stunned world to question, "*WHY?*"
Dante's inferno replaced the tiny village
Destruction was everywhere, nothing left to pillage

The village was wiped right off the map
While our national conscience took a long winter's nap
The president's planes had accomplished their mission well
They transformed the peaceful village into an instant Hell

When the massacre ended thousands lie mangled and dead
Unarmed civilians and babies snuggled in their bed
Then soldiers came, like robotic slaves
They bulldozed the bodies into mass graves
Hoping that the world wouldn't see enough to remember
The holocaust that happened on the twentieth of December

The Far Left Takes On The Far Right: An Open Letter To Patrick J. Buchanan

By: Rosemarie Jackowski / December 12th, 2004

Dear Mr. Buchanan:

Though you and I are on the opposite ends of the political spectrum, I sometimes find myself agreeing with you. I will take this opportunity to thank you for your support of third parties.

Today, as I read your column, I was disturbed by some of the ideas that you put forward. In your December 8 article about the United Nations, in World Net Daily, you state:

> *"...As for adding six new members to the council, that is the first step en route to an inevitable demand for veto power for all six. Russia, Japan and India are already insisting upon it. When granted, and gridlock ensues with 11 nations having a veto, there will come a clamor for diluting or abolishing the veto power altogether.*
>
> *For the hidden agenda of the United Nations, the International Criminal Court, the WTO and the Kyoto Protocol is to curtail America's freedom to act in its own interests and to midwife a world government erected on a one-man, one-nation, one-vote principle.*
>
> *Under a global democracy, India and China, with 2.5 billion people, would be the dominant powers, and peoples of color, five-sixths of all mankind, would enter a claim for a more equitable distribution of the world's wealth now held by that shrinking one-sixth of all mankind that is of European descent. Global democracy is the death of the West...."*

    ••• ――― •••   ••• ――― •••   ••• ――― •••

You imply that the veto power, currently held by the five permanent members of the Security Council, should be maintained. Think about that. Why should any one nation have veto power over the rights of the rest of the world? That is so undemocratic. Veto power should have never been given to any member. The veto power and any preferential treatment given to any member state should be eliminated. I oppose any preferential treatment with one possible exception. The weight of a member state's vote could be inversely proportional to the number of weapon systems of that nation. That system would give nations that lack military power increased voting power. There are two advantages to that proposal. It would discourage militarization and also be one step toward global equity.

In the next paragraph you say that *a one-man, one-nation, one-vote principle* is against America's interests. Ah, finally an admission from a right-winger that the fundamental principles of democracy are a detriment to America's interests. Thank you for putting that on the record. Those on my end of the political spectrum have been saying that for years. We need a little more democracy and a little less radical predatory capitalism.

The U.S. has a long record of using military force to prevent democracy throughout the world. I often site our government's actions in Iran in 1953 as just one of many examples. If, as you state, *"Global democracy is the death of the West."*, maybe it is time to plan for the funeral.

Respect for the International Criminal Court is necessary for global order. Membership should not be optional. Any nation, charged with a crime against international law, should be subject to the court's findings. If a nation chooses to not participate, that nation should be tried in absentia. A verdict should be rendered. The rule of law should prevail.

Also, numerous civil cases need attention in the International Court of Justice. For more than twenty years, the victims of the most horrific act of industrial negligence in history have been crying out for justice from their legal quagmire. Could it be that

U.S. corporations know how to game the system? Will the people of Bhopal ever receive justice? What about the people of Diego Garcia? What about the people of Panama? The international system of justice needs to be revised and strengthened. The U.S. should join the world community and give up its status as a rogue state.

The statement in your column that really disturbed me, enough that I am skipping my lunch to write to you, is your statement about *"peoples of color"* entering a claim for more equitable distribution of the world's wealth. I know that you did not intend any racial undertones in that statement. Unfortunately, the racial undertones are there, intentional or not...not only racial undertones but an imperialistic and xenophobic slant, too.

How could anyone be opposed to equitable distribution of the world's wealth? The only fair way to distribute the wealth and/or natural resources on the planet is on a per capita basis, with adjustments for climate etc. The people living in the tropics don't need energy for heating but the Canadians do. The fact that the United States has been using more than its fair share of the Earth's resources, has been a major global problem for a long time. Missing from your column are the legal or moral principles, which would justify an inequitable distribution of the earth's wealth. It is only by military power that we can take more than our fair share. In my mind, that is convincing evidence that the U.S. is following an undemocratic policy of Radical Predatory Capitalism.

     ••• — — — •••   ••• — — — •••   ••• — — — •••

A Holiday Wish List

By: Rosemarie Jackowski / December 6th, 2004

Dear Santa,

I hope that you have had a good year. It seems like a long time since I last sent you a letter. I am sure you know that things have not been going very well. Our country has made this a time of war on Earth and bad will toward all. Please do not hold that against all of us. Some of us have tried very hard to work for peace and show good will to our brothers and sisters. Unfortunately, there are not enough of us who really care.

Here is my wish list. I want Ralph Nader to be president and William Blum to become Secretary of State. I want Phil Donahue and Vladimir Posner to be given a new three-hour-long talk show. There is now an anchor position available at CBS. Could that job please go to Peter Mansbridge?

Santa, is there something that you can do about all of the war toys and violent video games? I am sure that you will not be putting any of them in children's stockings.

Please help all of the homeless people. Give every one of them a warm house to live in. Could you please make sure that everyone has health care. If you don't help, 45,000 people in the United States will die needlessly next year. A single payer system would be nice. Also a raise in the minimum wage would be big help. I know that you pay your elves a livable wage. While you are at it, could you please cancel all student loans?

The United States has harmed many people all around the world. It is very important that all of those who are victims of U.S. policies be paid reparations.

I really wish that when I wake up on Christmas morning, I will read in the newspaper that New England has seceded and that Texas has been given back to its rightful owner and is now, once again, part of Mexico. Florida, Georgia, and North and South Carolina should be given to the Iraqi people. We have contaminated their land with depleted uranium so we should give them some of our land that is not quite so contaminated. Of course, the rest of the country should be returned to the Native Americans.

Santa, please don't believe anything bad that you have heard about me. I have been very good all year. In fact, I have been so good that when I was arrested, the police said that we were the nicest people that they had ever taken into custody. I promise that when I am arrested again next year, I will be just as polite to the policeman as I was this year.

Say, *"Hello"*, to Mrs. Claus and the elves for me.

Your friend,
Rosemarie

   ••• ——— •••   ••• ——— •••   ••• ——— •••

No, Virginia, The Earth Is Not Flat...They Just Believe It Is

By: Rosemarie Jackowski / November 20th, 2004

Shocking as it may be, there are still those who believe that we are slaughtering people in Iraq because of 9/11. Then there are those who still believe that Iraq had WMDs. Also there are many who believe that we are fighting for *our freedom,* or to spread democracy. We are at war to keep us safe. That is what the government tells us, so it must be true. There are also those who believe that we are fighting for oil for our people.

WRONG, WRONG, WRONG. It may seem like a waste of effort to, again, address the 9/11 connection to the war, but someone better do that. The evidence to disprove the 9/11 argument for the war is readily available. Just read PNAC, written years before 9/11, or better yet, read *Blowback* by Chalmers Johnson. It, too, was written before 9/11 and explains how U.S. foreign policy would threaten all of us at home and abroad.

What about the argument that we are fighting for our freedom and to spread democracy? The facts speak for themselves. Are we more *"free"* now? And about the democracy explanation, remember Iran in 1953. Remember how the U.S. destroyed the democracy there. History proves that the U.S. is not above killing, in order to prevent democracy in the Middle East and elsewhere.

What about the argument that we are fighting in order to keep our country safe? Having become one of the most feared nations on the planet should dispel that argument. Our government has painted a target on the back of every U.S. citizen in many ways. For example, most areas in the U.S. are of mixed use, civilian and military. That means that most population centers are legitimate military targets. Even in some of the smallest towns and most rural areas, there are military contractors or subcontractors. How many military functions took place in the Twin Towers? Think about it.

What about the oil connection? Well, yes, oil is a consideration but the story does not end there. It is not oil for the people that the government wants. The need to increase profits from the oil for the corporations is the big motivation.

It is the quest for profits that causes war. It is just that simple. It is not some murky, complex ideological difference between Islam and Christianity. I need a bumper sticker that says, *"It's not about Christianity. It's about Capitalism."* Before it was about oil, it was about banana plantations. In the future, when there is no more oil, it will be about something else...maybe clean water or broccoli. The choice is an easy one...either expose capitalism for what it really is, or leave a legacy of endless wars, exploitation, and death for those who come after us.

These facts are so well known that it is almost embarrassing to restate them here. I will, no doubt, take a lot of flak for stating what is so obvious in this article, but it is important to consider the mindset of such a large percentage of the U.S. population. As badly as I want to shout, *"There is no 9/11 connection"*, I want even more loudly to shout, *"They think there is"*. If *they* think there is a connection, then that issue has to be addressed. If half of the population thought that the Earth was flat, then the issue of the flatness or the roundness of the planet would have to be discussed.

During an interview back in the early 1990s, Colonel David Hackworth is quoted as saying, *"In war some people die, and some people get rich."* Col. Hackworth is not a member of the anti-war movement. Indeed, he is a highly decorated military officer, definitely not a pacifist, just a realist who opposes the current war. The point is that no matter where you are on the *anti-war pro-war curve*, there are reasons to oppose the war in Iraq.

Actually the use of the word *"war"* is incorrect. How can there be a war if only one side is armed? How can a nation, which has already seen its military destroyed, be at war? If one side has DU, robotic assault weaponry, massive tools of terror and every kind of weapon that can possibly be imagined, and the locals are defending themselves with small homemade weapons, can this be called a

   ••• ––– •••   ••• ––– •••   ••• ––– •••

"war"? In the most recent, caught-on- tape war crime, the unarmed Iraqi civilian was killed because he was breathing. When breathing is interpreted as an act of aggression, it is time to examine the Pentagon's Rules of Engagement. This is a slaughter, genocide on a grand scale.

What the U.S. is doing in Iraq is a moral, legal, and diplomatic failure but beyond that, it is also one of the biggest strategic blunders in military history. Wars can be won or lost. The relevant question that no one is asking is, *"How do you win a slaughter?"* The simple answer is that a slaughter can never be won. Even if the U.S. killed every civilian in Iraq, would that be a win? Face it, the U.S. has already lost in Iraq. The killing will continue, but there will never be a victory for the U.S. There will never be a victory for the U.S. in Iraq because the entire world, with the exception of those in the U.S. (where the news is tightly controlled), has seen what the U.S. has done. The whole world is watching. Whispers of, *"Never again,"* are being heard from every corner of the globe. The international image of the U.S. will be tarnished for generations. Unlike previous atrocities committed by the U.S., this one was caught on tape.

In the anti-war classic, *War is a Racket*, the author, while discussing the cause of war states: *"...A few profit, and the many pay. But there is a way to stop it. You can't end it by disarmament conferences. You can't eliminate it by peace parleys at Geneva. Well-meaning but impractical groups can't wipe it out by resolutions. It can be smashed effectively only by taking the profit out of war...".* Those words were written by USMC General Smedley Butler in 1935.

Write In Nader...The W.I.N. Campaign

By: Rosemarie Jackowski / August 22nd, 2004

In spite of rumors to the contrary, Democracy is not dead yet. There is still a glimmer of hope. Spread the word, make yard signs, write letters to the editor, tell all your friends. Get the message on every blog site. We are taking our country back. Who are we? We are the vast majority of voters. We are the ones who say, *"None of the above,"* on Election Day. We are the ones who will write in *"NADER"*.

Even after a campaign of dirty tricks by the Democrats, a series of almost fatal blows to democracy by the Republicans, the disappearance of the last investigative journalist in the mainstream media, and a conspiracy to silence Third Parties and Independents by the Commission on Presidential Debates, guess what. We are still here. We are not only still here, but on November 2nd we will prove that the pen is mightier than the sword.

This time Nader will get enough votes to affect the outcome of the election. The WIN CAMPAIGN will change the course of history. In states where *"NADER"* does not appear on the ballot, there will be a campaign to write him in. This is strictly a grassroots movement. The official Nader campaign has not yet endorsed it.

There will be weeping and wailing about this campaign from the Republicrats. The Republican Party has the most to fear, because the Nader platform is a direct assault on most Republican policies. The Republicans should have foreseen this before they followed their leader into the quagmire. The Democrats should have foreseen this before they followed the Republicans into the quagmire.

And just for the record, the WIN CAMPAIGN was inspired by the Democratic platform committee. Remember, the DPC refused to include in the platform a statement that the invasion of Iraq was a *"mistake"*. That is the moment when the Democratic Party lost its Base. For many, that was the last straw. No one who opposes war can, with a clear conscience, vote for Kerry. The ABB voters should examine their consciences before they go into the voting booth.

The strongest argument in support of Nader is his platform. The way to convince undecided voters is to show them all three platforms (Nader, Democratic, and Republican) with the names omitted. The Nader platform wins almost every time. If voters were voting on platform issues only, Nader would win in a landslide.

Think about it. What is the percentage of votes needed to make an impression in Washington? In this election, 3 or 4 percent might be the magic number. There is growing support from Independents, Greens, Libertarians, Reformers, and Socialists. They will join with disenfranchised Democrats and Republicans to create a *perfect storm* of dissent on Election Day.

If everyone, who is not satisfied with either Bush or Kerry, gets 10 or 12 voters to write in NADER, we will reach our goal. The goal is to *"win"* the election, but not necessarily in the usual sense of the word. The objective is to bring fundamental change to the political and economic systems. This goal is much more important than winning just one election. The goal is to change the course of history. This is the only way to stop pre-emptive wars, to bring a single-payer health care system to all, to bring a livable wage to all workers, and to protect the environment. This is the only way to end corporate rule. If there is another way, let's hear about it.

It is more important now, than at any other time in recent history, to show the Washington elite that the citizens have a voice. We will not allow our country to be controlled by corporations and unelected Washington think tanks any longer.

Don't throw your vote away. A vote for Nader is a vote for change. A vote for either Bush or Kerry is a vote *"to stay the course."* We might not get the president of our choice this time, but if our votes change the course of history, we will get the president of our choice next time, and then WE ALL WIN.

••• ——— •••   ••• ——— •••   ••• ——— •••

The 9/11 Commission Report Is A Masterpiece Of Obfuscation

By: Rosemarie Jackowski / August 18th, 2004

The 9/11 Commission Report has raised the art of obfuscation to new heights. Its name should be changed to The Red Herring Report, or The Ostrich Report. The 9/11 Commission members should be retired and replaced with people who would do something to end the violence.

Author-historian William Blum states in his book *Rogue State* that he could end terrorism. He writes, "*... If I were the president, I could stop terrorist attacks against the United States in a few days. Permanently. I would first apologize—very publicly and very sincerely—to all the widows and orphans, the impoverished and the tortured, and all the many millions of other victims of American imperialism. Then I would announce to every corner of the world that America's global military interventions have come to an end. I would then inform Israel that it is no longer the 51st state of the union but—oddly enough—a foreign country. Then I would reduce the military budget by at least 90% and use the savings to pay reparations to the victims and repair the damage from the many American bombings, invasions and sanctions. There would be more than enough money. One year's military budget in the United States is equal to more than $20,000 per hour for every hour since Jesus Christ was born...*"

I confess. I have not read all 567 pages of the 9/11 Commission Report. I have watched the Congressional Hearings on C-Span. Kristen Breitweiser, in her testimony before the Congressional Committee said, "*...The jigs up...*" (C-Span2, Aug. 17, 2004, 10:45 a.m.). It would have been a move in the right direction if she had been referring to U.S. actions around the world, but the context of her statement showed that she believes that the tragedy of 9/11 was a failure of Intelligence. The testimony of other family members of victims, Stephen Push and Mary Fetchet, indicated a greater willingness to recognize that 9/11 was a failure of Diplomacy. In Mary Fetchet's testimony, she stated, "*...Foreign policy is the core of*

182

The most compassionate act, that any of us can do in support of the 9/11 families, is to inform others about the government's international policies that led to 9/11. I have not seen any member of Congress or any member of the commission mention the part that U.S. foreign policy played in the tragedy. Ignoring the role that U.S. foreign policy played in causing the tragedy of 9/11, is like ignoring the elephant in the middle of the room.

Authors have been predicting a 9/11 type of attack for many years. Chalmers Johnson wrote his book, *Blowback*, before the attack happened. The CIA has been using the term *"blowback"* for decades because they knew that there would be a violent reaction to U.S. foreign policy. It was common knowledge. In view of this, how can it be that not one of our elected officials in Washington could foresee the event?

There are two possibilities...first; none of our representatives was smart enough to think in terms of cause and effect. That is hard to believe. There is a better explanation. Some of them DID know. They did not know the time and place of the attack, but they had to know that an attack would be the inevitable result of U.S. foreign policy. If they didn't know before 9/11, they surely have to know now.

Still, even today, there is no one in Washington suggesting that the time has come for a major change in U.S. foreign policy. One can only conclude that the U.S. government has made the conscious decision, that the loss of thousands of lives in the U.S., and millions of lives in other countries, is an acceptable part of the cost of doing the business of the Empire.

Capital Punishment Because You Couldn't Pay The Premium

By: Rosemarie Jackowski / August 14th, 2004

None of us will ever forget the September 11 tragedy. The final death toll was 2,976 (CBSNEWS.com).

Today, in the United States, 45 million people have no health insurance. Those without access to health care are at increased risk of death. According to an Institute of Medicine report, 45,000 U.S. citizens die each year because they are without health insurance. That is like having a 9/11 tragedy every 30 days. It is even worse than that, because this is a tragedy that we are imposing on ourselves. We are the terrorists who are blocking the clinic door. This is *death by legislative inaction,* or *death by corporate lobbying,* or *death because your government likes corporations more that it likes you,* or *Capital Punishment because you couldn't pay the premium.* Call it whatever you like. The fact is that 45,000 of us will die needlessly within the next 12 months unless we do something about it.

When we vote in November, one of the important issues to be considered is whether we should continue to impose these 45,000 deaths on U.S. citizens each year. The question is, *"Which candidate will keep us safer from those deaths which are caused by lack of access to health care?"* A universal, single-payer system is urgently needed. U.S. citizens are already paying for it, but the money is being siphoned off by insurance companies, HMOs, and the pharmaceutical companies.

The Bush platform does not include health care for all. The Kerry platform does not include health care for all. Only one major candidate includes a single payer, universal, health care system for all in his platform. That is Ralph Nader.

United States Foreign Policy Exposed

By: Rosemarie Jackowski / August 7th, 2004

The official position of the government of the United States is that it invaded, and now occupies, Iraq because the U.S. wants to spread Freedom and Democracy in that region of the world. Only someone who does not know about U.S. escapades since WW 2, could ever fall for such a line of propaganda. Fortunately, many people around the world remember what happened when Iran DID have a Democracy. On August 19, 1953, Dr. Mohammed Mossadegh, the duly elected prime minister was overthrown in a CIA coup. The government of the United States took such action because Prime Minister Mossadegh wanted Iran's oil to be used for the people of Iran. Even back then, the official U.S. policy was that the oil under Iran's sands was the property of U.S. corporations. The U.S. coup in Iran was so successful, that soon after it, in 1954, the CIA was sent on a similar mission to Guatemala. Guatemala did not have oil, but it had something else that a U.S. corporation was coveting. The United Fruit Company wanted the soil upon which bananas were growing. The CIA accomplished its mission in Guatemala, and another Democracy was obliterated.

For the past 50-plus years, the foreign policy of the United States, has taken the U.S. military around the globe, exploiting one nation after another. This *creeping imperialism* is causing concern all around the world. Author Chalmers Johnson states that the U.S. has 700 bases in 130 countries. What the U.S. cannot get with bribes and indecent maneuvers in the UN, it gets with bombs. An updated list of the countries that the U.S. has bombed since WW 2, as compiled by historian William Blum follows: China (1945-46), Korea (1950-53), China (1950-53), Guatemala (1954), Indonesia (1958), Cuba (1959-60), Guatemala (1960), Congo (1964), Peru (1965), Laos (1964-73), Vietnam (1961-73), Cambodia (1969-70), Guatemala (1967-69), Grenada (1983), Libya (1986), El Salvador (1980), Panama (1989), Iraq (1991-2004), Sudan (1998),

Afghanistan (1998-2003), Yugoslavia (1999). This is only a partial list. It does not contain the countries, such as Colombia, where the secret U.S. army of mercenaries is doing the bombing. It does not list locations that were bombed and contaminated as testing sites, such as Vieques.

Which country will be next? Will it be Korea or Cuba, France or Finland? No one knows, and no one is safe until U.S. foreign policy is changed. In studying the William Blum list of bombed countries, it becomes apparent that countries with a brown-eyed population are at increased risk. If you are not frightened yet, you have not been paying attention to recent world history. During the March 13, 2002 White House press conference, President Bush stated that all options were on the table. This comment, by President Bush, came just days after the Pentagon's Revised Nuclear Posture Review was leaked to the *Los Angles Times*. In it, the Pentagon named seven countries that were potential targets of a U.S. NUCLEAR strike. Still not frightened? You better check out what happened to the people of Diego Garcia, when the U.S. military decided that it wanted their island as a military base.

For all of the people around the world, who are waiting for the citizens of the United States to stop this 50-year long killing and bombing spree, I have bad news. Most U.S. citizens know more about their favorite sports teams than they do about foreign policy. Do not look to them for help. Somehow, along the way, something happened to the U.S. national conscience. When the Pentagon used the dehumanizing term, *"collateral damage,"* to refer to the slaughter of civilians, not one member of the press ever spoke up and said, *"No, not collateral damage. Those are human beings"*. Even worse, the press adopted and repeated, without question, the language of the Pentagon. U.S. citizens never got to see the face of the little Iraqi girl, killed by a U.S. cluster bomb. The press is so deeply embedded in the government, that the Truth no longer exists.

It is time for the international community of nations to respond to military actions in which civilians are killed. A Global Campaign of Zero Tolerance is needed. When the first bomb hits the first civilian, that action should set off an immediate and automatic response from the entire world community. There are many non-violent responses that would be appropriate, such as economic boycotts etc., until the offending nation gives up all of its weapons. More than 13,000 Iraqi civilians have been killed since March 20, 2003.

The movement to safeguard humanity will have to come from outside of the U.S. In the U.S. there is no debate, no opposition party, and no dissent. Those who did try to raise their voices at the Democratic National Convention, in Boston, were silenced and caged. The United States will never bring Freedom and Democracy to the rest of the world. It cannot even bring freedom to Boston, or Democracy to Washington D.C., where the citizens still don't have voting representation in Congress.

The Secret That The Government Kept For 30 Years

By: Rosemarie Jackowski / August 1st, 2004

Currently the United States has so many military bases around the world that it is almost impossible to get an accurate count of the exact number. Author Chalmers Johnson states that the U.S. has 700 bases in 130 different countries. The history of the acquisition of many of these bases shows a clandestine, nefarious, and cruel attitude toward the people who originally occupied the locations where the bases now are. The official word used by the Pentagon to describe bases in other countries is *"Footprint."* What could be more arrogant than one country putting its footprint on another sovereign nation?

The history of the U.S. base on Diego Garcia is of special interest now. The base was built by Halliburton and commissioned on March 20, 1973. Exactly 30 years later, on March 20, 2003, the Shock and Awe bombing campaign was launched from Diego Garcia. This base has been a recent topic of discussion in the British House of Commons. The people who inhabited Diego Garcia, until the United States forced them to leave, are now seeking justice. Court documents reveal that a policy of ethnic cleansing by the U.S. government has continued for over 30 years.

The following are quotes from a CBS *60 Minutes* special on Diego Garcia:

- *"Total evacuation. They [the U.S.] wanted no indigenous people there."*

- *"[T]hey weren't allowed to take anything with them except a suitcase of their clothes..."*

- *"The people of Diego Garcia say they left paradise and landed in hell when they were dumped in the urban slums of Mauritius..."*

188 ••• ——— •••   ••• ——— •••   ••• ——— •••

- *"No one helped them resettle or pay for the homes they lost. They were forced to become squatters in a foreign land. Jeannette Alexis' family was one of the last to leave: 'My father was told that we had to leave the island because the Americans were moving in and it wasn't safe to remain on the island anymore.'"*

- *"officials ordered their pets to be exterminated. They were gassed with exhaust fumes from American military vehicles."*

- *"And for the next 30 years, the world never knew what happened to Diego Garcia's original people."*

- *"No outsiders are allowed onto Diego Garcia, so this secret stayed hidden until one of the exiled islanders, Olivier Bancoult, started organizing his community. So three years ago, Olivier traveled to London to take the British government to court. His big break came when he and his lawyer, Richard Gifford, found secret documents that had recently been declassified that described the agreement between the United States and British governments to build the base on Diego Garcia. These British documents reveal that colonial officials thought no one would notice if they deported the islanders. Another British document confirms that 'evicting the people and leaving the island to the seagulls' was done at the request of the United States. It reads: 'The United States Government will require the removal of the entire population of the atoll by July.' Uncovering the paper trail brought Gifford and Bancoult a stunning victory. Britain's highest court ruled that deporting Diego Garcia's native population was illegal. So last August, the islanders appealed directly*

The Fifth Amendment of the U.S. Constitution sets forth the principle of fair compensation in eminent domain cases. It could be argued that the Diego Garcia case is not covered by the U.S. Constitution because Diego Garcia is not part of the U.S. That very argument would make the case for reparations because that is precisely the point. Diego Garcia is not a part of the U.S. and therefore the U.S. government never had any rights of ownership there. The belligerent occupation of Diego Garcia by the U.S. has been a violation of fundamental principles as laid out in the U.S. Constitution, a violation of international law, a violation of U.S. treaties, and a violation of human rights.

Does the secret history of the United States in Diego Garcia show that U.S. foreign policy is based on the belief that some people are inferior? Is this a racist policy? Or is it just that human rights will always be secondary to the desires of the U.S. military? The former inhabitants of Diego Garcia want the freedom to occupy their own country. This freedom has been taken away by the U.S.

Do not look for the facts of this clandestine operation in any U.S. history textbook. Our government has been masterful at keeping the secret for 30 years. Some documents were declassified and then found in 1999 only because of a judicial process in Britain. (Now additional information is available on CBS News's website. Correspondent Christiane Amanpour reported on this story for CBS.)

Thus far, the U.S. has made no apology, has paid no reparations, and has permitted no judicial remedy. Will the government of the U.S. ever allow the people of Diego Garcia to return to their homeland? Will the people of the United States join with others around the world and work toward the immediate closing

    ••• ––– •••   ••• ––– •••   ••• ––– •••

of the base at Diego Garcia? Will the U.S. government clean up the hazardous materials on the base, and pay reparations to all of the original inhabitants? Will a filmmaker ever produce a documentary of this, one of the greatest stories of our time? Will lawyers in the U.S. answer the call and write amicus briefs, so that justice, which has been delayed for so long, will now be possible? Will a team of international lawyers ever assemble, and bring this case to the World Court? After more than 30 years, it is now time to let the people of Diego Garcia go home.

(Update: The documentary *Stealing A Nation*, by award winning journalist John Pilger was broadcast for the first time in October 2004. It is now available on the internet.)

To Vote, Or Not To Vote

By: Rosemarie Jackowski / July 28th, 2008

To vote, or not to vote, that is the question. Many have already decided to sit this election out. Some came to that decision for philosophical reasons. Some will no longer vote for the 'lesser of the evils', but not all of the candidates are evil. The list of Presidential candidates includes some good ones and some others. There is a variety to chose from. A partial list- Barr, McCain, McKinney, Moore, Nader, and Obama.

There are some things worse than not voting. One of them is casting an uninformed ballot. That is the worse of the worse. It cancels out the vote of a citizen who has been paying attention. A mandatory voters test is not a good idea, but voters should be encouraged to follow their consciences when deciding to vote, or not to vote.

Please, don't vote if you don't know your candidate's position on all of the important issues. Don't vote if you don't have a working knowledge of U.S. foreign policy.

For your convenience, the brief test below should help answer the question of whether or not you are an informed voter. Many who have taken the test have scored a perfect 10. There are no trick questions. It's really very easy.

<u>Test Your Foreign Policy I. Q.</u>

Answer the following 10 questions and rate your knowledge of United States foreign policy.

1. What historic event occurred at No Gun Ri in 1950?
2. How did the United States acquire its military base in Diego Garcia?
3. Which official United States agency coined the term "blowback" and predicted a 9/11- type attack?
4. How many countries have been bombed by the United States since World War 2?

5. Name the U.S. Marine Corps General who exposed the connection between U.S. military actions and the quest for corporate profits? (Hint) He wrote his expose' in 1935.
6. How many U.S. military bases are located in foreign countries?
7. How many foreign nations have military bases in the U.S.?
8. What is the name and location of the U.S. military base that has gained worldwide attention because its mission is the training of terrorists?
9. What is the name of the U.S. official who gave Saddam Hussein permission to invade Kuwait?
10. When did the U.S. start the war against Iraq?

Rating your F.P.I.Q. Test

A score of 10 correct means you are to be congratulated. You win the "Informed Citizen of the Week" award. Hopefully you will be invited to make a guest appearance on the Bill O'Reilly show, to be followed by appearances on Hannity & Colmes, Larry King, Oprah, Meet the Press, and the Colbert Report. More likely, you will be banned from ever speaking in the media. Congratulations, you are an informed voter.

A score of 9 answers correct, you are much better informed than the average citizen.

A score of 8 correct, not bad, but you need a little help.

If you scored 7, it's time to hit the books. Suggested readings would include: *A History of the United States* by Howard Zinn, *Killing Hope* by William Blum, *Blowback* by Chalmers Johnson, *The Seven Deadly Spins* by Mickey Z, *Confessions of an Economic Hit Man* by John Perkins, *On the Justice of Roosting Chickens-Reflections on the Consequences of U.S. Imperial Arrogance* by Ward Churchill, and *The New Rulers of the World* by John Pilger. Also see the Robert Fisk war photos of civilian victims in Iraq. These photos have been censored out of most of the U.S. media. If you had only 6 right answers, you need a lot of help. Please don't vote unless you do a lot of studying first.

If you had 5 or less correct, you probably work for, or get your information from, FOX, NBC, CBS, or ABC. Every time that you vote, you might be canceling the vote of an informed citizen. You need to reassess your right to participate in a democracy. No democracy can survive if the citizens are not well informed. Stay in bed on election day.

The Answers

1. No Gun Ri is the location of a U.S. massacre of civilians in South Korea. Survivors report that more than 400 unarmed men, women and children were gunned down by the U.S. military.
2. Diego Garcia was acquired in the 1970s. The island was a paradise that had been inhabited for generations. The United States and Great Britain were complicit in crimes against humanity by the expulsion of the native population.
3. "Blowback" is the term coined by the CIA in 1954. It has been well known since 1954 that U.S. foreign policy would result in blowback.
4. Since WW 2, the United Stated has bombed: China 1945-46, Korea 1950-53, China 1950-53, Guatemala 1954, Indonesia 1958, Cuba 1959-60, Guatemala 1960, Congo 1964, Peru 1965, Laos 1964-73, Vietnam 1961-73, Cambodia 1969-70, Guatemala 1967-69, Grenada 1983, Libya 1986, El Salvador 1980s, Nicaragua 1980s, Panama 1989, Iraq 1991-99, Sudan 1998, Afghanistan 1998, Yugoslavia 1999. This list has been compiled by historian/author William Blum.
5. U.S.M.C. General Smedley D. Butler wrote *War Is A Racket* in 1935.
6. Author Chalmers Johnson states that there are more than 700 U.S. bases in foreign countries.
7. None
8. Fort Benning in Georgia is the location of the *School of the Americas.* Congress quietly renamed it *The Western Hemisphere Institute for Security Cooperation* in an attempt to sanitize its image. Around the world it is known as *The School of Assassins.*
9. Ambassador April Glaspie.
10. March 20, 2003 is the date of the start of the Shock and Awe bombing campaign and is often erroneously given as the date of the start of the war. The war really began with U.S. bombings in 1991.

     ••• ––– •••   ••• ––– •••   ••• ––– •••

Christmas On Mill Street

*Based on a true story - for the young and the young- at- heart.
Dedicated to children and grandchildren everywhere.*

By: Rosemarie Jackowski / 2009

It was December 24, 1914. The smell of cookies baking in the oven of the old coal stove filled the kitchen. Momma had just added another kettle of hot water to the big round metal wash tub. The tub was placed in front of the stove because that was the warmest place in the house.

Brother Stevie and Poppa were outside repairing the chicken coop. Suddenly Poppa came inside. As he brushed the snow off his coat, he whispered something to Momma. It was something about the *'old country'* and war. Momma seemed sad and whispered that she would pray for peace. Then Poppa went back outside to finish his work.

Brother Julius had already taken his bath. Now he was sitting on the floor playing with the dog.

Momma said, *"Little Tony it's your turn. Get in the tub. You want to be cleaned up for Christmas, don't you?"*

Little Tony quickly took off his clothes and hopped into the tub.

Momma was busy taking the cookies off the flat metal baking sheets. Julius rushed up to the table and grabbed one of the cookies. Momma said, *"Julius, I saw that. We need to save these cookies for tomorrow."*

Little Tony said, *"I want a cookie too".* Momma said, *"Tony, wash your knees. They are still dirty."* Tony said, *"Momma, can I get out of the tub now? I'm clean. Look, even my toes are all crinkled up. That means I have been in the tub a long time."*

$$\cdots --- \cdots \qquad \cdots --- \cdots \qquad \cdots --- \cdots$$

Momma just smiled. Tony then asked why toes and fingers get crinkled up in the tub.   Momma said that it was because the skin absorbs water. Little Tony said that he would have to think about that. He was always asking questions. He wanted to learn as much as he could because he recently had to quit school. He was only eight years old, but now he had to go to work instead of being with the teachers and all of the other kids.

Finally Momma told Tony to get out of the tub. He did. He quickly put on his long underwear and his special sweater. Momma had knitted the sweater for him. It was red with one white sleeve. Momma did not have enough red yarn so she finished the sweater with white yarn instead.

Momma told Little Tony that it was time to go upstairs to bed. He kissed Momma and then he patted the dog on the head and went into the parlor. He quickly pulled one of his socks off his wiggling toes. He hung the sock on a small hook on the fireplace. Then he scampered up the steps.

Upstairs he could hear a noise. Bang, bang, bang. Oh, that must be Santa on the roof, Tony thought. He looked out the window. The noise was just the wind blowing on the outhouse door. Bang, bang, bang.

Little Tony knelt by the window. He looked up in the night sky and said a prayer asking God to bless all the children and all of the poor people in the whole entire world. Then he hopped into his bed. He was so excited. Maybe when he woke there would be something from Santa in his sock - maybe even a candy cane. After all, he had been a very good boy. He always helped his Momma and Poppa. Every Saturday he scrubbed the outhouse. Sometimes he would go to a nearby farm and help take care of the horses.

It was very quiet when Tony woke up on Christmas morning. Everyone else was still sleeping. Little Tony climbed out of his bed and quietly tiptoed down the stairs. He peeked around the corner and looked toward the fireplace. He saw that something was in his sock. Santa had left a present for him! He was so excited that he

   ••• ––– •••   ••• ––– •••   ••• ––– •••

tripped on the corner of the rug and slid on his belly clear across the parlor floor. He grabbed his sock off the fireplace hook. He put his hand in the sock and felt something. What could it be? It was round. Maybe it was a baseball. He pulled it out. He had never received such a precious gift before in his entire life. It was an orange - a beautiful orange. It was the most beautiful thing he had ever seen.

Little Tony ran up the stairs and woke everyone up. He had to show them his wonderful gift. Tony promised himself that he would keep the precious orange forever. He would never eat this wonderful prize. He kept it inside his sweater when he went out. He kept it in his bed when he went to sleep. He gently put it on his pillow when Momma said that he had to take a bath. Every day he polished it by rubbing it on his sweater. Eventually most of the orange part was worn off. It was now a white orange.

One day, after his bath, Tony went upstairs to look at his white orange. It was gone!   Tony looked under the bed. Maybe it had rolled off the pillow. He crawled under the bed. It was not there. He looked everywhere. The precious orange was gone. He knelt down by the window. He tried to be brave. He would not cry. Maybe if he said a prayer, God would make the orange come back. As Tony was praying he looked up in the dark sky and there he saw a new white star that twinkled with an orange glow. Oh, there is my orange he squealed! Now all of the children of the world can see my beautiful orange.

Tonight, look up into the dark night sky, and if you have been very good, you will see Little Tony's bright star. It is the one that twinkles with an orange glow.

To all my children - Goodnight. Sleep well, and know that you are loved.

••• ▬ ▬ •••   ••• ▬ ▬ •••   ••• ▬ ▬ •••

Archival Photo dated 1991 - Main Street, Bennington, Vermont

 ••• ––– •••   ••• ––– •••   ••• ––– •••

Part Three

Court Record of the Sentencing Hearing which was separate from the Trial.

The words give only a very small glimpse into what really took place. No printed words can convey the intensity of emotion felt in the Court that day.

··· --- ···   ··· --- ···   ··· --- ···

State of Vermont vs Rose Marie Jackowski 452-4-03 Bncr Sentencing Hearing - 10-7-2004

STATE OF VERMONT
BENNINGTON COUNTY, SS.

State of Vermont   )
) Bennington District Court
        v.   )
) Docket No. 452-4-03 Bncr
Rose Marie Jackowski,   )
            Defendant.   )
____

SENTENCING HEARING

As recorded on October 7, 2004, at

Bennington District Court

Before the Honorable David T. Suntag

TRANSCRIBER: Donna Gould

APPEARANCES:

ON BEHALF OF THE STATE OF VERMONT:

    DANIEL M. MCMANUS, ESQUIRE

ON BEHALF OF THE DEFENDANT:

    STEPHEN L. SALTONSTALL, ESQUIRE

I N D E X

EXAMINATION

Witness   Page

ANDREW SCHOERKE
    Direct Examination by Mr. Saltonstall   6-10

NATALIE HOLLY
    Direct Examination by Mr. Saltonstall   10-17
    Redirect Examination by Mr. Saltonstall   19

ELLIOT ADAMS
    Direct Examination by Mr. Saltonstall   21-24

CHRISTINE JACKOWSKI
    Direct Examination by Mr. Saltonstall   24-27

E X H I B I T S

PLAINTIFF'S EXHIBITS

Exh. No/Description   Page Ident.   Page Rec'd.

(None)

DEFENDANT'S EXHIBITS

Exh. No/Description   Page Ident.   Page Rec'd.

A - Photographs   13

```
 1                    (October 7, 2004)

 2    (Tape No. 100)

 3              THE COURT:  Please be seated.  Good

 4    morning, Mr. Saltonstall.

 5              MR. SALTONSTALL:  I wasn't sure whether

 6    it was our time yet, Judge.

 7              THE COURT:  It's yours.  Okay.  This is

 8    the matter of State v. Jackowski.  We are here for a

 9    sentencing hearing after a jury verdict of guilty on a

10    disorderly conduct charge.  There have been no post

11    trial motions filed, and so we are here for sentencing.

12    Mr. McManus, do you intend to introduce any evidence

13    today?

14              MR. MCMANUS:  No evidence, your Honor.

15              THE COURT:  Mr. Saltonstall, will you be

16    introducing any evidence?

17              MR. SALTONSTALL:  Yes, your Honor, we do

18    have some witnesses.

19              THE COURT:  Okay.  How many?

20              MR. SALTONSTALL:  Four plus my client

21    would ha -- like to elocute.

22              THE COURT:  Four -- yes.  Four plus or --

23              MR. SALTONSTALL:  Four plus, yeah.

24              THE COURT:  Okay.  And State know who

25    they are?  Have you let them know?
```

```
 1              MR. SALTONSTALL:  No.

 2              THE COURT:  Well, let's start and see how

 3   we do.

 4              MR. SALTONSTALL:  All right.  I'd like to

 5   call Andy Schoerke, please, your Honor.  That's spelled

 6   S-c-h-o-e-r-k-e.

 7              THE COURT:  Okay.  Sure.

 8              ANDREW SCHOERKE,

 9      called as a witness by and on behalf of the

10      Defendant, having been first duly sworn, was

11      examined and testified as follows:

12              COURT OFFICER:  Please be seated and

13   state your name for the record.

14              DIRECT EXAMINATION

15   BY MR. SALTONSTALL:

16      Q.     Would you state your name for the record,

17   please?

18      A.     My name is Andrew C. Schoerke.

19      Q.     And Mr. Schoerke, where do you live?

20      A.     I live at 212 Middle Road in Shaftsbury,

21   Vermont.

22      Q.     And are you retired?

23      A.     That's correct, sir.  I'm a retired naval

24   officer.

25      Q.     And are you a member of any peace
```

```
 1   organizations?

 2        A.      I'm a member of the Chapter 44 Veterans for

 3   Peace.

 4        Q.      Would you tell the Judge what your military

 5   service has consisted of?

 6        A.      I entered the military in June of 1956.  I

 7   was commissioned an -- an ensign.  On active duty, I

 8   served two years with Heavy Attack Squadron One on board

 9   the USS Forrestal, USS Independence.  I was a bombardier

10   navigator.  Our mission was to drop the atomic bomb in

11   the event of war.

12        Q.      And did you --

13        A.      After that --

14        Q.      Go ahead.

15        A.      -- I -- I entered the Ready Reserve Program

16   and was what is commonly called a weekend warrior for 20

17   years at the Naval Air Station, Willow Grove,

18   Pennsylvania serving under the direction of the Naval

19   Intelligence Command.

20        Q.      And when did you end that service?

21        A.      I retired from service in September of 1979

22   with a rank of captain.

23        Q.      Do you know Rose Marie Jackowski?

24        A.      Yes, I do.

25        Q.      How long have you known her?
```

1   A.   I've known Rose Marie Jackowski for

2   approximately three years.

3   Q.   And in what context have you gotten to know

4   her?

5   A.   I know Rose Marie from our meetings with the

6   Veterans for Peace chapter in southern Vermont. I've

7   witnessed with Rose Marie for peace on the four corners

8   on many occasions. I have attended grassroots peace

9   meetings with Rose Marie and marched with Rose Marie in

10   peace parades here in Bennington.

11   Q.   And have you spoken with her from time to

12   time about her views?

13   A.   Yes, I have.

14   Q.   And what have you learned?

15   A.   I learned that Rose Marie has a deep sense

16   of moral values. I -- I know from talking with Rose

17   Marie that she has a deeply held sense in the integrity

18   and sanctity of human life. I know from talking about

19   military service that Rose Marie is keenly dedicated to

20   the oath that she swore when she became an officer in

21   the United States Air Force. I am also aware of Rose

22   Marie's deeply held conviction about the -- the use of

23   authority and its commensurate value with the rule of

24   law.

25   Q.   And what have you learned from Rose Marie

```
 1    about -- both from talking with her and observing her

 2    about her motivation in connection with this offense for

 3    which she's been convicted, the offense of disorderly

 4    conduct?

 5         A.    If I recall correctly, when I first met Rose

 6    Marie, she was -- she was appalled and -- and clearly

 7    moved about the impact that the sanctions were having on

 8    the people of Iraq, specifically with the death of one

 9    half million Iraqi children as reported by the United

10    Nations World Health Organization.  That -- that -- that

11    to me was quite a -- quite an overwhelming burden for --

12    for Rose Marie's conscience to bear.

13              And her following -- her follow-on

14    activities in the -- our local grassroots peace and

15    justice community was dedicated to preventing additional

16    impact, additional killing and maiming of Iraqi

17    children, in particular and in general innocent

18    civilians that would be impacted by this war.

19         Q.    And what's your view of her sincerity in

20    that regard?

21         A.    I -- I'm not too sure how I can attest to

22    her sincerity other than the fact that I know Rose

23    Marie's strength in -- in adhering to normally accepted

24    norms of behavior was very strong and very long held and

25    it was quite -- quite revealing, to say the least, when
```

 1   Rose Marie stood with -- with me and others the day

 2   after the -- the war started in Iraq.

 3   And clearly I think from what I -- from what

 4   I believe, Rose Marie's intention was to -- to act as a

 5   fire bell in the night, to -- to rouse the local

 6   citizens, friends and neighbors to the -- to the impact

 7   that this war was going to have.

 8   MR. SALTONSTALL: Thank you very much.

 9   THE COURT: Mr. McManus?

10   MR. MCMANUS: No questions, your Honor.

11   MR. SALTONSTALL: Your Honor, we'd like

12   to call Natalie Holly to the stand, please.

13   NATALIE HOLLY,

14   called as a witness by and on behalf of the

15   Defendant, having been first duly sworn, was

16   examined and testified as follows:

17   COURT OFFICER: Please be seated and

18   state your name for the record.

19   THE WITNESS: My name is Natalie Holly.

20   DIRECT EXAMINATION

21   BY MR. SALTONSTALL:

22   Q.   Ms. Holly, could you speak right up because

23   that microphone doesn't amplify anything.

24   A.   Sure.

25   Q.   Where do you live, Ms. Holly?

1   A.   I live in Hoosick Falls, New York.

2   Q.   And are you also retired?

3   A.   Yes, I am.

4   Q.   And what did you do when you worked?

5   A.   I worked for the New York State Department

6 of Health and Communicable Disease Control, HIV

7 infection, AIDS and tuberculosis control.

8   Q.   And how did you get to know Rose Marie

9 Jackowski?

10   A.   I first met Rose Marie at a -- at a Quaker

11 meeting probably three or four years ago. We talked

12 at -- at that time and a couple of times about our --

13 our convictions.

14   Q.   And did you later become friends?

15   A.   Yes.

16   Q.   Have you had a chance to formulate a view of

17 Rose Marie's character?

18   A.   I think so, yes.

19   Q.   Would you tell the Judge what that is?

20   A.   I think that Rose Marie, more than anyone I

21 know, lives by her beliefs on a daily basis. She I

22 believe follows a highest form of patriotism, which is

23 to try to maintain the principles and the ideals upon

24 which the country was founded by speaking out when she

25 thought that those principles and ideals were being

1   violated. She -- I think she's one of these people that

2   has really dedicated her life and her energy and her

3   heart to just causes.

4   Q.   Okay. Were you present at the demonstration

5   at which she was arrested?

6   A.   Yes, I was.

7   Q.   Were you also arrested?

8   A.   Yes.

9   Q.   Did you happen to observe her while she was

10   standing there in the -- at the four corners with her

11   sign?

12   A.   Yes. I was standing fairly close to her,

13   and I -- I did -- I did observe her and looked at her a

14   couple of times. I -- I looked at her a couple of times

15   because a little concerned because I saw that she was

16   crying, and I wasn't sure why she was crying, but I -- I

17   did feel concern.

18   Q.   Did you ask her about that later?

19   A.   I did later asked her why she was crying,

20   and she said two things. She said that she had never

21   before -- she had never before broken the law let alone

22   disobeyed a -- an authority figure, and the other reason

23   was because she was very, very focused on the deaths

24   that were occurring in Iraq at that moment as we stood

25   there during Shock and Awe and, in particular, the lives

 1   of children that were being taken.

 2   Q.   Now, did you have an opportunity to look at

 3   certain photographs of children with her and discuss

 4   them?

 5   A.   Yes. I, first of all, saw the --

 6   Q.   Wait a sec.

 7   A.   Oh.

 8   Q.   I'm going to show you what has been marked

 9   Defendant's A. Could you tell the Court what these

10   photos are of?

11   A.   These photos are of children who have been

12   severely injured and/or have died in Iraq since March

13   19th, 2003. Particular ones are from the Robert Fiske

14   web site, who's an independent journalist who's been in

15   Iraq for many, many months, British.

16   Q.   And -- and could you tell us, please, tell

17   the Court what the discussion you had was with Rose

18   Marie with respect to these photos and what they depict?

19   A.   Okay. Rose Marie asked me if I could bring

20   to her house photos that we'd both seen on -- on a

21   couple of different web sites, but she didn't have a

22   printer, so I printed them and took them to her house.

23   I re -- I remember it vividly. We sat on

24   her front steps, it was a nice day, and I put the folder

25   with the photos on her lap, and she opened it and looked

 1   at a couple of photos and started weeping. I was

 2   envious because I -- I'm not able to cry like her. The

 3   one photo in particular I think that has affected Rose

 4   Marie the most is this child with her head blown off.

 5   THE COURT: That's enough. It's not been

 6   admitted. Please let's not demonstrate it. Thank you.

 7   THE WITNESS: Oh, I thought it was. I'm

 8   sorry.

 9   Q.   And were -- in your view, were the injuries

10   and deaths depicted in these photos of Iraqi children

11   part of the -- Rose Marie's motivation in doing what she

12   did?

13   A.   I think it was all of her motivation. I --

14   she has been from then and to this day, every day

15   focused on these deaths. Every time I talk to her,

16   every time we go to -- to a talk or a -- or a

17   demonstration of some kind, she -- she brings up --

18   she -- this is her subject.

19   MR. SALTONSTALL: At this time, your

20   Honor, I'd offer Defendant's A.

21   THE COURT: Mr. McManus?

22   MR. MCMANUS: Your Honor, I object.

23   Photos from a web site, the worldwide web is a transient

24   type of -- I don't know the source of these photos, and

25   frankly, we're not retrying this case. This is

1   something that might have been more appropriate for the

2   trial, but I don't see it as being appropriate for

3   sentencing hearing.

4   THE COURT: Is there any question, Mr.

5   McManus, about Ms. Jackowski's sincerity in her views

6   about the war and killings?

7   MR. MCMANUS: No, that -- that's not

8   being -- there's no relevance to this whatsoever.

9   THE COURT: There's really no need for

10 the photographs, Mr. Saltonstall. There's no question

11 about her view.

12   MR. SALTONSTALL: So you're excluding

13 those, Judge?

14   THE COURT: Yes. I mean, it seems to me

15 they're rather sensational now.

16   MR. SALTONSTALL: All right. May I leave

17 them with the Court for purposes of appeal?

18   THE COURT: Approach, please.

19   (The following took place at the bench.)

20   THE COURT: Why?

21   MR. SALTONSTALL: What's that?

22   THE COURT: Why?

23   MR. SALTONSTALL: Because the Court

24 should take --

25   THE COURT: Pictures of dead children,

```
 1    blown-up children (inaudible).

 2                    MR. SALTONSTALL:  We respectfully

 3    disagree on the admissibility of them, Judge, and I want

 4    to appeal that.

 5                    THE COURT:  (Inaudible) haven't seen

 6    them?

 7                    MR. SALTONSTALL:  What?

 8                    THE COURT:  Why would you put pictures of

 9    dead (inaudible)?

10                    MR. SALTONSTALL:  May I make an offer of

11    proof of them then?  May -- you want to look at them?

12                    THE COURT:  (Inaudible) pictures of dead

13    blown-up children.

14                    MR. SALTONSTALL:  Yes.

15                    THE COURT:  They're not going to be

16    admitted.

17                    MR. SALTONSTALL:  Okay.  May I leave them

18    in the court file for purposes of appeal?

19                    THE COURT:  (Inaudible) seal them up and

20    put them in an envelope (inaudible) --

21                    MR. SALTONSTALL:  All right.  All right.

22                    THE COURT:  -- (inaudible) please.

23        (The following took place in open court.)

24    BY MR. SALTONSTALL:

25        Q.    Were you arrested at the same demonstration
```

```
 1    that Rose Marie was arrested at --

 2         A.    Yes.

 3         Q.    -- that we're here about today?

 4         A.    Yes.

 5         Q.    And were you taken to the police station?

 6         A.    Yes, I was.

 7         Q.    And were you detained at the police station

 8    in a jail cell?

 9         A.    Yes.

10         Q.    Did you see that Rose Marie Jackowski was

11    also detained at the same police station in a different

12    cell?

13         A.    Yes.

14         Q.    How long were you and she detained?

15         A.    Several hours.

16              MR. SALTONSTALL:  I don't have any

17    further questions for this witness.

18              THE COURT:  Mr. McManus?

19              MR. MCMANUS:  None, thank you.

20              THE COURT:  Ms. Holly, can I ask you were

21    you prosecuted?  Did they bring a charge against you?

22              THE WITNESS:  Yes.  Yes.

23              THE COURT:  What happened to your case?

24              THE WITNESS:  Well, we came to court and

25    our lawyer gave us our options.  The others, not Rose
```

    1   Marie --

    2   THE COURT: No, I'm talking about you.

    3   THE WITNESS: -- and we chose the

    4   diversion.

    5   THE COURT: You went to a diversion

    6   program?

    7   THE WITNESS: Yes.

    8   THE COURT: What did you wind up having

    9   to do?

   10   THE WITNESS: I paid $250.

   11   THE COURT: To?

   12   THE WITNESS: To the -- the -- the

   13   diversion center.

   14   THE COURT: Um hum.

   15   THE WITNESS: And I did 30 hours of

   16   community service.

   17   THE COURT: I see. What did you do for

   18   community service?

   19   THE WITNESS: I worked at the senior

   20   center in Bennington.

   21   THE COURT: All right. Was this

   22   something that you chose to accept? You could have

   23   rejected it yourself?

   24   THE WITNESS: I could have.

   25   THE COURT: I see. Okay.

1   THE WITNESS: I wish I had.

2   THE COURT: You can step down.

3   MR. SALTONSTALL: May I question the

4   witness about what you've asked her, Judge?

5   THE COURT: You can.

6   REDIRECT EXAMINATION

7   BY MR. SALTONSTALL:

8   Q.   Would you do the same thing now?

9   A.   Would I plead guilty?

10   Q.   Yes.

11   A.   No. I -- I'm very much impressed with Rose

12   Marie's courage in -- in going through with the trial.

13   I feel that --

14   Q.   Why didn't you --

15   A.   -- being arrested and then pleading guilty

16   really weakened, if not reversed, my stand that day and

17   I regret it. If I'd ha -- I just -- at the time I

18   didn't have the courage or stamina to -- to go true with

19   a trial.

20   MR. SALTONSTALL: Okay. I don't have any

21   further questions.

22   THE COURT: Just to be clear, you pled

23   guilty? I thought you said it was the diversion which

24   would have been before such a --

25   THE WITNESS: We had to sign a paper that

1 we were guilty in order to get the diversion.

2   THE COURT: I see. But you've not been

3 convicted of an offense, have you?

4   THE WITNESS: Well, I --

5   THE COURT: The process allowed you to

6 not be convicted of a --

7   THE WITNESS: From what I understand,

8 we -- we had been convicted, but after two years, our

9 record will be sealed.

10   THE COURT: Was it diversion?

11   THE WITNESS: Yeah.

12   THE COURT: Okay. All right. Thank you.

13 All set. You're all set.

14   MR. SALTONSTALL: I don't have any

15 further questions.

16   THE COURT: Mr. McManus, anything

17 further? Okay. Thank you.

18   MR. SALTONSTALL: Elliot Adams, please,

19 your Honor.

20   ELLIOT ADAMS,

21   called as a witness by and on behalf of the

22   Defendant, having been first duly sworn, was

23   examined and testified as follows:

24   COURT OFFICER: Please be seated and

25 state your name for the record.

1   THE WITNESS: Elliot D.S. Adams.

2   DIRECT EXAMINATION

3   BY MR. SALTONSTALL:

4   Q.   Mr. Adams, where do you live?

5   A.   I live in Sharon Springs, New York.

6   Q.   And what do you do for work?

7   A.   I am a partner in A & H Forest Management, a

8   logging firm.

9   Q.   Are you a member of a peace organization?

10   A.   A number. I'm a member of Veterans for

11   Peace, I am a member of FOR, Fellowship of

12   Reconciliation. We also have a local peace group.

13   Q.   And did you serve in the armed forces?

14   A.   I did. I volunteered in the late '60s,

15   volunteered for the Army, volunteered for Vietnam,

16   volunteered to be a paratrooper, served in Vietnam with

17   the 173rd as an infantry paratrooper, was medevaced to

18   the hospitals in Japan, spent a while in the hospitals

19   in Japan, redeployed through the 2nd Division in Korea,

20   then joined -- then went airborne in -- in Alaska with

21   the -- with the 10th Mountain Division.

22   Q.   And have you gotten to know Rose Marie

23   Jackowski?

24   A.   I have met her at demonstrations and talked

25   to her con -- on the phone and e-mailed.

1   Q.   All right. I understand that you've

2 prepared a very short statement that you'd like to -- to

3 read in connection with this sentencing, and if the

4 Court allows, I'd like you to do that now.

5   THE COURT: As long as it's directed to

6 Ms. Jackowski and the sentencing, that will be fine.

7   MR. SALTONSTALL: It is, Judge.

8   THE COURT: All right. Thank you.

9   THE WITNESS: Thank you, your Honor.

10 "Your Honor, I, like Rose Marie, am a veteran. We know

11 patriotism demands that we put our country before

12 ourselves. I have not known Rose Marie long. As fellow

13 vets, as fellow patriots, we speak a common language.

14 We know that serving our country calls for more than

15 saluting the flag. It calls for a hard love. It

16 demands -- it demands of us that we act, even against

17 our self-interests, even against the wishes of our

18 neighbors, for what we believe to be good for the

19 country.

20   Rose Marie acted in the great American

21 tradition. She acted as a true patriot putting her

22 country first. From my conversations with Rose Marie,

23 it is clear that she knows the horrific costs of the

24 losses being borne by the civilians in Iraq, that she

25 feels that pain to her bones, that she is driven by that

1   pain.

2   I know heroism personally from combat.

3   Heroism requires ignoring your own well-being to

4   accomplish a greater goal. As soldiers, Rose Marie and

5   I both know that a tunnel vision that blocks out risks

6   that others see clearly is often needed to complete the

7   mission. She was a real hero when she refused to allow

8   the risk to herself to deter from the goal of alerting

9   all of us, the public, to the horrors we were raining

10   down on the Iraqis, especially poignantly, the

11   civilians.

12   Our great democracy puts demands on -- on

13   its citizens. We must take responsibility for all the

14   acts of our government. In our democracy, it is not

15   sufficient to vote. We must be a guiding hand for our

16   government every day. To be citizens, true patriots, we

17   must make our voices heard when we believe our

18   government is wrong. At times we will have to shout.

19   Rose Marie felt her voice was not loud

20   enough to be heard and that the wrongs being done were

21   horrific, so the true American citizen, in her own

22   patriotic way, she shouted. She acted in the long

23   tradition of Bennington as a true daughter of

24   Bennington.

25   Your Honor, whether or not the jury liked

 1   what she did or how she did it, I ask that you recognize

 2   that my friend and fellow vet acted, unlike most of us,

 3   as a true patriot would. She acted heroically and she

 4   acted as a true American citizen."

 5   MR. SALTONSTALL: Thank you. I don't

 6   have any further questions, your Honor.

 7   THE COURT: Mr. McManus?

 8   MR. MCMANUS: Nothing. Thank you.

 9   THE COURT: Thank you.

10   THE WITNESS: Thank you.

11   MR. SALTONSTALL: Thank you. Your Honor,

12   our last witness is Christine Jackowski, the daughter of

13   Rose Marie Jackowski.

14   CHRISTINE JACKOWSKI,

15   called as a witness by and on behalf of the

16   Defendant, having been first duly sworn, was

17   examined and testified as follows:

18   COURT OFFICER: Please be seated and

19   state your name for the record.

20   THE WITNESS: Christine Theresa

21   Jackowski.

22   DIRECT EXAMINATION

23   BY MR. SALTONSTALL:

24   Q.   Ms. Jackowski, where do you live?

25   A.   I live in North Greenbush, New York now.

 1   Q.   And are you married?

 2   A.   I'm married.

 3   Q.   And your husband's name is?

 4   A.   Christopher VerWey.

 5   Q.   Do you have a child also?

 6   A.   We do. We have an eight-month-old son. His

 7   name is David.

 8   Q.   Okay. And what do you do?

 9   A.   I'm a stay-at-home mom.

10   Q.   Okay.

11   A.   Finally.

12   Q.   Did you do work before that?

13   A.   Yeah, I -- previously I worked with a lot of

14   nonprofit organizations, program development, but most

15   recently I worked for Fleet Bank doing business analysis

16   work for them.

17   Q.   Okay. And did you go to college?

18   A.   I did. I went to college here in Bennington

19   at Bennington College, which is what brought us to this

20   community.

21   Q.   You and your mom?

22   A.   Me and my mother, yes.

23   Q.   When did you graduate?

24   A.   I graduated in 1989.

25   Q.   And were you living with your mother here in

```
 1   Bennington when you went to Bennington College?

 2        A.      Yes, I did.  I lived at home and was a part

 3   of the community and a part of the college, which is

 4   kind of unusual in this town, but I feel very strong

 5   ties to both.

 6        Q.      And you were a scholarship student, as I

 7   understand it?

 8        A.      I was.  Thankfully, yes.  I was able to make

 9   my dream come true of going to Bennington, yes.

10        Q.      Okay.  I -- I understand that you have also

11   written a statement of two paragraphs, and if the Court

12   allows it, I'd ask that you do that now.

13               THE COURT:  Please.

14               THE WITNESS:  Thank you.  "I've known

15   Rose Marie Jackowski my whole life.  One thing that I

16   can tell you about my mom is that she never does

17   anything without 100 percent commitment.  She fought

18   tire -- tirelessly when I was a girl to seek justice for

19   victims of deadbeat dads.

20               When I was 13, she took me to my first

21   peace rally in Central Park.  There we saw hundreds of

22   people coming together for peace and justice.  It was

23   there that she bought me a button that said Question

24   Authority, and that became a bit of a motto in our home.

25               Over the past three decades, my mother's
```

 1 │ unwavering commitment to children took focus on the

 2 │ children of Iraq who, we all agree, do not deserve the

 3 │ horrors of war. I urge us all to wish the same warmth,

 4 │ safety and love for the children of Iraq as we do for

 5 │ our own children. Recently I became a mom myself, and I

 6 │ feel so lucky and proud to have a mom like Rose Marie.

 7 │ She is an example of bravery for us all.

 8 │   I ask the Court to remember my mother's

 9 │ long-time commitment to peace and making this world a

10 │ better place. We love her so much, and for that I ask

11 │ the Court to sentence her with time served. Thank you."

12 │   MR. SALTONSTALL: That concludes our

13 │ evidence, your Honor.

14 │   THE COURT: Mr. McManus, you want to ask

15 │ any questions?

16 │   MR. MCMANUS: No, thank you.

17 │   THE COURT: Okay. Thank you. Concludes

18 │ the evidence. All right. Mr. McManus, I'll -- I'll

19 │ hear from you, then Mr. Saltonstall, I know your -- your

20 │ client wishes to exercise her right of elocution. You

21 │ can do that in whatever order you wish.

22 │   MR. MCMANUS: Your Honor, the State

23 │ recommends a sentence of 200 hours' community service to

24 │ be performed in the community of Bennington, that being

25 │ someplace that will actually benefit the community

 1   affected by Ms. Jackowski's actions, be it the library,

 2   the hospital. The one thing which would not be

 3   acceptable would be for a peace group, something that

 4   does not benefit directly the community.

 5   In the alternative, the State would ask

 6   that Ms. Jackowski be sentenced to the reparative board.

 7   She can meet with the board and the board, which is

 8   comprised of community members, can determine what an

 9   appropriate sentence would be for the community

10   affected.

11   It's -- from the evidence, it's clear

12   that Ms. Jackowski has strong personal beliefs, but she

13   was misguided in how she expressed those beliefs. The

14   way she expressed them, granted it got her this trial

15   and all the publicity, and I'm sure that that's a bonus

16   to her; however, it affected a lot of people's lives in

17   a negative way, and it didn't really do much of anything

18   to further her goal other than the -- the media coverage

19   here today.

20   If we were dealing with a group of white

21   supremacists or a group of people advocating war and

22   advocating the bombing of Iraq in the middle of the

23   street, I doubt we'd have the same amount of people

24   coming up here and testifying for leniency. I mean,

25   maybe -- probably her intentions were good, but in no

1   way do her actions reflect that. It's clear she broke

2   the law. It never was a question that she broke the

3   law.

4   The testimony here today, it seems that

5   they're trying to gather leniency because, in her mind

6   and their mind, she broke the law for a good purpose.

7   However, as the State contends, there were abundantly --

8   abundant options for her to get her message out in a

9   positive way, a way that didn't affect the community and

10   a way that, quite frankly, would probably have made a

11   better -- bigger impact than this.

12   If this were a true case of civil

13   disobedience, Ms. Jackowski probably would have just

14   pled and taken the sentence that had come to her.

15   That's true civil disobedience. That's the real --

16   that's Martin Luther King, that's Ghandi. This is not

17   true civil disobedience. This is just a means to get

18   media attention and to create a buzz. Media's going to

19   cover it, it's a sexy story, it's, you know, something

20   that's going to sell papers.

21   But the fact of the matter wa -- is she

22   did commit the act of disorderly conduct. She's already

23   been found guilty. People were affected. People were

24   angry. There are people here who support her actions.

25   I'm sure there are many in the community that disagree

1   with her actions.

2   Regardless, what the Court needs to focus

3   on is the conduct, and the conduct isn't the most

4   egregious, by far, that comes through here. However, a

5   sentence of time served does not address the conduct

6   properly. The Court should think about the community

7   affected, keep that in mind when sentencing, and again

8   the State recommends either 200 hours or a set amount of

9   community service to be performed in the community or

10   the re -- reparative board where the community can

11   address the conduct on their own.

12   THE COURT: Mr. McManus, concerning all

13   the other cases of people who had been arrested other

14   than Ms. Jackowski, my understanding was that all of

15   those cases actually went through diversion and avoided

16   court --

17   MR. MCMANUS: I almost -- I'm sorry. I

18   didn't mean to cut you off.

19   THE COURT: -- and whatever was required

20   of community service, there were no convictions here by

21   plea or otherwise; is that right?

22   MR. MCMANUS: When a person goes through

23   the diversion process, that does not result in a

24   conviction. I am not certain that all that were

25   arrested completed diversion. I almost want to say that

 1 there was a college student or two that may have left

 2 the jurisdiction before completing their obligations,

 3 but I think the vast majority of the people arrested on

 4 that day did complete diversion. Ms. Jackowski was

 5 referred to diversion. She --

 6   THE COURT: And to complete diversion,

 7 they -- you have to accept the offer to go do diversion,

 8 sit with the board --

 9   MR. MCMANUS: Yes.

10   THE COURT: -- make a determination

11 whether (inaudible) accept what they ask you to do, do

12 it and then your case is simply dismissed.

13   MR. MCMANUS: If you accept --

14   THE COURT: Right. And complete it.

15   MR. MCMANUS: -- and do what they ask,

16 yes.

17   THE COURT: Yeah. Okay. (Inaudible).

18   MR. MCMANUS: And Ms. Jackowski

19 declined --

20   THE COURT: Okay.

21   MR. MCMANUS: -- the diversion referral

22 and came here and wanted a trial for obvious reasons.

23   THE COURT: All right. I understand.

24 All right. I just wanted to find out about the other

25 cases. All right. Mr. Saltonstall, any -- whatever

1   order you wish (inaudible).

2   MR. SALTONSTALL: Okay. Before talking

3   about Rose Marie, I just want to address a few things

4   that the deputy state's attorney said that I think are

5   really inappropriate. Comparing Rose Marie Jackowski to

6   white supremacists is just wrong. White supremacists

7   stand for hate and division in our society.

8   Rose Marie Jackowski was, in her view,

9   standing up for people of color, children in Iraq, and

10 to compare someone who's dedicated her life to peace

11 organizations to white supremacists I think is more than

12 over the top. I think it's grossly inappropriate.

13   Martin Luther King and his followers went

14 to trial many times and appealed many convictions and

15 they made some good law. The deputy state's attorney is

16 just wrong about that. I was in the civil rights

17 movement myself. I know that from experience.

18   To say that Rose Marie Jackowski did this

19 just to create media attention for herself is also

20 wrong. She wasn't the only one that got media

21 attention. The deputy state's attorney got plenty of

22 media attention, and I didn't see him running away from

23 the news cameras after he won the trial.

24   As a matter of fact, Rose Marie Jackowski

25 hasn't done this for herself, she did it for a cause.

1   She's 67 year -- years old, Judge. She lives on social

2   security as she testified. She has no money. The Court

3   granted her in forma pauperis motion before the trial.

4   She has no prior criminal record. She stands convicted

5   of disorderly conduct, and while every -- every offense

6   is serious in some sense, this is one of the least

7   serious in terms of possible penalties in the criminal

8   code.

9   As you know, Judge, she blocked traffic

10   for a period of time of about a half an hour, as I

11   understand it, while engaged in -- in the protest

12   against the war. She's testified that she was motivated

13   out of sincerity to protect the Iraqi children. People

14   here have testified on sentencing about that, and even

15   the deputy state's attorney in final argument, unlike

16   his argument today, said that he believed that my client

17   was sincere.

18   To tell you a little bit about her

19   background, your Honor, Rose Marie was born in a coal

20   mining region of Pennsylvania in 1937. Her father had

21   to quit school in the second grade to work, and he

22   shoveled coal for 50 cents a ton during the Depression,

23   so that was the kind of poverty that my client grew up

24   in.

25   She started work herself at age ten in a

1   sweatshop while going to school, and later she worked

2   while in high school as a newspaper stringer. She went

3   to college at night while working during the day for TV

4   Guide, of all things, and also for General Electric in

5   the steam turbine department.

6   She did not graduate from college, but

7   she got enough credits so that she -- at least in those

8   days, she was able to teach school in New Jersey, which

9   she did for a number of years, and then motivated out of

10   patriotism, she joined the United States Air Force, went

11   to Officer's Candidate School and ultimately was --

12   received an honorable discharge.

13   At that point, your Honor, she moved to

14   Florida. She started to teach again, and then after

15   that, she worked in -- for Pratt & Whitney, a defense

16   contractor in -- as an engineering and aeronautical

17   aide.

18   At age 30, her life changed when she was

19   raped while walking home from dinner, and she got her

20   first taste of the criminal justice system then. There

21   was no prosecution by the rapist. Even though she

22   identified him, he was never questioned by the police,

23   and she was told at that time this is just the kind of

24   thing that men do every Saturday night, you don't want

25   to hurt this guy, do you, or words to that effect.

1   She moved to Rochester. There she worked

2   for General Dynamics, another defense contractor, and

3   married and had her daughter Christine whom you saw

4   testify here today. One day, she was abandoned by her

5   husband who took her car and all her money and leaving

6   her poverty stricken, and the justice system failed her

7   again at that time. She never received any

8   court-ordered child support from her husband. When she

9   went to family court to try and get an order of support,

10   the judge was reading the newspaper and, after she had

11   said her piece, told her to leave.

12   As you heard, Judge, her daughter

13   Christine was accepted to Bennington College I think at

14   age 16, she was one of the youngest people to go there,

15   and Rose Marie moved with her daughter to Bennington so

16   they could live together and save money.

17   Ironically, in June of 2000, Rose Marie

18   had another unsatisfactory dealing with the State when a

19   State of Vermont dump truck carrying a full load of logs

20   severely injured her after rear-ending her, and that's

21   left her unable to work, and it made her -- made it very

22   painful, Judge, for Rose Marie to sit during the trial,

23   and I can attest to that.

24   The other thing that happened was that on

25   the first day of trial, the local welfare department

```
 1   wrote Rose Marie a letter of intent to cut off her food

 2   stamps, and what happened -- I looked into this.  The

 3   welfare department, I guess it's called PATH now, had --

 4   someone in the department had read newspaper coverage of

 5   the case where it said that Rose Marie was writing

 6   articles, and they jumped to the incorrect conclusion

 7   that she was making money from this activity when she

 8   received no money for her writing.  This is writing for

 9   the peace movement on web sites.  And after her trial, I

10   had to intervene with the State so that her food stamps

11   would be reinstated.

12             Obviously what you have to decide here,

13   Judge, is what is appropriate punishment for someone

14   who's -- who's elderly, who has physical problems, who

15   has no previous record, who was sincere in her protest

16   of the Iraq war, somebody who's had a very hard life.

17   She served her country as a veteran of the Air Force.

18   Her prior experiences with the justice system have been

19   characterized by injustice, and someone also who this

20   Court has found to be indigent and who can't pay a fine.

21             As was testified to, Judge, Rose Marie

22   did spend several hours in police custody in jail.  She

23   was in a jail cell, and we think an appropriate sentence

24   would be time served in this case.  Apparently she's the

25   only one to get a conviction out of this demonstration
```

1   and she's the only one to do any time.

2   If the Court feels that additional

3   punishment is necessary, Rose Marie has asked me to ask

4   you to impose another day or two of jail time. We don't

5   feel that someone like her needs to be on probation, we

6   think it's a waste of resources for the State, and she

7   again has asked me to ask you -- to tell you, Judge,

8   that she has conscientious scruples against performing

9   mandatory State-ordered community service because in her

10   view, that furthers what she believes to be an unjust

11   system and bolsters State power.

12   And with respect to the recommendation of

13   a reparative board, she believes that there's no need to

14   make reparations, that although she broke the law, what

15   she did was -- was right, and she also feels that

16   there's a distinction between doing something at the

17   behest of the government, the government ordering her to

18   do something versus accepting something that the

19   government is doing to her such as arresting her and

20   putting her in jail.

21   Judge, we're also asking you to stay in a

22   sentence pending appeal pursuant to Rule 30(a). As I

23   look at the rule, I think that the stay is mandatory

24   except -- in this type of case except for an order of

25   probation which it says the Court may stay the sentence,

 1   and we're asking you to do that.

 2   In terms of the merit of our appeal, you

 3   know a lot about Rose Marie. As I mentioned in

 4   chambers, I think that we -- we do have a meritorious

 5   appeal. It's far from frivolous. We objected at the

 6   bench to your Honor's instruction on specific intent

 7   which was based, of course, on Vermont Supreme Court

 8   cases, particularly the instruction on practical

 9   certainty.

10   Because that -- the State's proposed

11   instructions were given to me over the lunch hour and I

12   couldn't go on-line to check them out, I did not see a

13   later case, state versus Trombley, which is at 174

14   Vermont 459, a 2002 case where they say that, "An act

15   intentionally -- when an act is charged as intentionally

16   done," in that case it was I think aggravated assault,

17   which it was here, "the model penal code makes a

18   distinction between an intentional act and an act

19   knowingly done. That is, there is a difference between

20   a knowing act and an intentional act."

21   And the practically certain instruction

22   only goes to a knowing act, and as your Honor recalls,

23   you gave both, and I think that's what happened in

24   Trombley, so we do feel that we have a meritorious

25   appeal and -- and ask you to stay any sentence that

 1   needs to be stayed.

 2   So to recap, your Honor, we think that in

 3   these individualized circumstances of Rose Marie, the

 4   kind of person that you've heard that she is, somebody

 5   who's never broken the law before, who's served her

 6   country, who did this out of good motives, that one day

 7   served in jail with a permanent conviction is punishment

 8   enough. We'd ask you to do that and to stay any

 9   sentence that needs to be stayed. We thank you very

10   much. Now Rose Marie would like to say a few words.

11   MS. JACKOWSKI: Your Honor, I want you to

12   know that I have deep respect for you, and I am asking

13   you to please don't ask me to do anything that would

14   in -- that would invalidate my active conscience because

15   I can't. I will not go against my conscience.

16   And I know Mr. Saltonstall made the

17   point, but I just want to repeat that I believe that

18   there is a real moral difference between having the

19   State or the government do something to me as opposed to

20   my doing something because the government tells me to.

21   And personally, I find the word

22   reparative very insulting because I don't think that the

23   criminal justice system should be based on humiliation,

24   and I think that in this case, that's what it would be.

25   And now I would like to read my statement, which is very

1   short. I know your Honor gets a little bit impatient,

2   so I timed this and I think -- I think it's about four

3   minutes.

4   "Your Honor, I would like to express my

5   gratitude to you, the prosecutor, Mr. McManus, members

6   of the Bennington Police Department, to my family,

7   especially Christine, and to all of those who support me

8   and, of course, especially Mr. Saltonstall. It is my

9   profound respect for the rule of law that brought me to

10   the four corners on March -- March the 20th of '03.

11   At the precise moment of my arrest, the

12   federal government of the United States was bombing

13   civilians. The bombing of civilians is a violation of

14   international law, a violation of U.S. treatise, a crime

15   against humanity and a war crime.

16   Now that same government is sitting in

17   judgment of many who have protested the war. Last week

18   in a court in Philadelphia, Lillian Willoughby, an

19   89-year-old deaf woman in a wheelchair, was sentenced to

20   prison," and I just would like to add here that Ms.

21   Willoughby chose prison rather than a $250 fine because

22   she felt the same way I do, that she didn't want to do

23   something that would invalidate her act of conscience.

24   "She had pro -- she had participated in a peaceful

25   protest.

 1   Also in Philadelphia, Andrea Ferrick, a

 2   22-year-old, was sentenced, and she just spent a week in

 3   solitary confinement, not even able to receive mail.

 4   She had also participated in a peaceful protest. All

 5   over this country, hundreds of those who have peacefully

 6   protested the war are now condemned by the government.

 7   The way this country is heading,

 8   eventually all people of peace will be behind bars. I

 9   am in solidarity with them and all others who have

10   resisted the government in the past or who will do so in

11   the future." And your Honor, I don't think that it's

12   been in the news, but I have been told that last

13   Saturday in Washington, D.C., I was not there, Michael

14   Berg, father of Nick Berg, was arrested along with about

15   30 members of veterans for peace. I mean, this is the

16   road this country is going down.

17   "Your Honor, it is with deep respect that

18   I voice some concerns. How can it be that a nation that

19   is in -- itself in violation of the law can then hope to

20   impose the rule of law on its citizens. I believe that

21   either the rule of law applies to everyone or also it

22   applies to no one. Even a nation as powerful as the

23   United States cannot have it both ways.

24   The fact that the government of the

25   United States is in violation of the law is a fact that

1   has been documented by many around the world. William

2   Blum," spelled B-l-u-m, "one of the world's leading

3   historians and also a former employee of the United

4   States State Department, has authored several books on

5   the topic, even naming one of his books about U.S.

6   foreign policy Rogue State."

7   Your Honor, I am not going to read all of

8   this, but I have here a copy of the indictment against

9   members of the United States government of 19 charges as

10   compiled by former U.S. Attorney General Ramsey Clark.

11   I also have here a statement entitled U.S. Lawyers Warn

12   Bush on War Crimes.

13   Also a statement of international law

14   from an organization that's accredited by the United

15   Nations. "And this brings out the extensive U.S. war

16   crimes in Iraq. This is just a small sample of

17   information that is easily available. Can all of these

18   reports be wrong? There are literally hundreds of

19   thousands of them."

20   I also have here an Associated Press news

21   clipping from prior to my arrest, and this is one of the

22   things that was on my mind. "I think everyone needs to

23   be reminded that the government of the United States was

24   threatening the use of nuclear weapons at the day and

25   time we were arrested, and the government had

1   consistently done that for about a year prior to our

2   arrest. To threaten the use of nuclear weapons is a war

3   crime even if you don't actually carry out that threat.

4   That is a war crime and a crime against international

5   law.

6   Your Honor, I believe that our government

7   will not regain its legal and moral authority until it

8   gives up its international life of crime and, in the

9   words of William Blum, is no longer a rogue state. It

10 is important to say here that the war in Iraq is not the

11 first violation of human rights and inter -- and

12 international law by the United States.

13   The abuse of people, people just like you

14 and me, started way back in 1492 and has been a

15 consistent pattern ever since. Talk to some native

16 Americans, especially now that Columbus Day is upon us,

17 talk to our black brothers and sisters, talk to the

18 people of Diego Garcia or Panama or Hiroshima or Cuba.

19 The list is endless.

20   As individual citizens, we all have

21 rights and responsibilities. I believe that it is the

22 responsibility of all citizens to resist any government,

23 anywhere, any time when that government is slaughtering

24 civilians. I and many other protesters that I know

25 would gladly spend the rest of our lives in prison if

1   only the United States would stop bombing civilians.

2   I have always been opposed to any form of

3   violence. Seeing the photographs of the bombed Iraqi

4   children has changed my life and has strengthened my

5   commitment to working for justice for those children. I

6   do not understand how anyone can stand by silently

7   knowing that civilians are being bombed.

8   Thousands who protested the war as I did

9   are being criticized, but to those people who are our

10 critic -- critics, I would ask what is the proper thing

11 to do? If you were walking down Main Street right now

12 and you saw a gang of thugs beating up a child and about

13 to murder her, should you write a letter to the editor

14 or should you call your congressman or maybe write a

15 pamphlet about how adults should interact with children?

16 Of course not.

17   When children are being slaughtered,

18 intervention of the most powerful, immediate and direct

19 kind is called for. What the other protesters and I did

20 should be criticized only for one reason. We all did

21 too little. To all of the people of Iraq, especially

22 those who have lost family members, I want to say here

23 today that I am sorry. I will try to do better in the

24 future.

25   Your Honor, I pray for the day when

1 factory workers join with farmers and police officers

2 join with poets and judges join with veterans in

3 protesting the illegal acts of our government. Now is

4 the time in history when silence is the greatest of all

5 crimes.

6   What happens to me here today is not

7 important. I only ask that you not ask me to violate my

8 conscience. Since the day of my arrest, more than

9 13,000 Iraqi civilians have been killed. That is

10 important. Thank you very much."

11   THE COURT: Mr. McManus, anything

12 further?

13   MR. MCMANUS: I was severely misquoted by

14 defense counsel, but I won't address it now.

15   THE COURT: Just trying to look at that

16 case you cited. But back to what we are here for. Ms.

17 Jackowski, I am not foolish enough to try to engage in a

18 debate with you about either your motives, the American

19 foreign policy or anything else we've been speaking of

20 today. I'm not going to do that.

21   Nor is there anybody here who's even

22 suggesting that you are not sincere in your beliefs.

23 Nobody in the state, nobody is suggesting that. Nobody

24 disagrees with that. The only disagreement has to do

25 with tactics, and in this light, the tactics violated

1   the law.

2   There is one other tradition I'd mention

3   because I know there's been some criticism apparently of

4   what the jury did and I need to speak for them. You

5   spoke of tradition and -- and I agree with what you had

6   to say and Mr. Saltonstall did, too, but one other

7   honored tradition in this country is the jury trial.

8   And 12 people from the community came

9   here and sat and listened and made a decision, and I

10 respect that decision because they were asked to follow

11 the law and listen and made that decision. We've been

12 doing that for hundreds of years too. That's why we're

13 here now. So we may criticize a lot of things, but

14 hopefully not what a jury decides.

15   What we are here for is the fact that

16 there's now been a conviction for the offense of

17 disorderly conduct. It is certainly not the most

18 egregious offense ever. It was, in essence, an

19 obstruction of traffic for about a half hour I'll take

20 that to be. People were disturbed who were waiting, I

21 guess. We don't really know, of course, who those

22 people were and where they were headed and whether it

23 was something important or urgent or not. We really

24 have no idea. It could have been just as easily it

25 could not have been.

1   The obstruction was the offense. You

2 were convicted of that offense, and what it did was

3 cause a harm of some sort to the community. Now, the

4 harm was not a great harm, but it was some. That's why

5 it's a crime.

6   And so the only question here is what

7 should be the sentence. I believe Mr. Saltonstall spoke

8 about sentencing only having to do with punishment. It

9 doesn't. If that was so, then we'd be done because you

10 were arrested and brought to a police station and held

11 in a cell for a number of hours, and if that's not

12 enough punishment for somebody who's never been through

13 it, I don't know what is.

14   So that solves that part of the

15 sentencing, but there's much more to sentencing.

16 Sentencing also attempts to address whatever harm there

17 was to the community and return to the community

18 anything that was taken.

19   In this instance, the community itself

20 was offended at some degree. That's why it was a crime.

21 And it seems perfect sense to me that those who should

22 be considering what should occur because of this and

23 setting out if there is anything more that needs to be

24 done members of the community. That's this type of

25 offense. It makes perfect sense.

1   And in fact, it allows you an opportunity

2   to speak with other individuals in the community and

3   communicate what you communicated today and discuss with

4   them again why you did what you did and then let them

5   decide whether anything more is appropriate.

6   One further thought. Everybody else that

7   was arrested that day, as I understand it, was

8   prosecuted and nevertheless offered an opportunity to

9   avoid the entire court process, which is what this

10   diversion thing was all about. I'm not suggesting you

11   should be treated more harshly because you chose not to

12   accept it. You have your beliefs. Again, they appear

13   to be sincere about why you did that.

14   But those other folks went through the

15   diversion program, they did not have to plead guilty in

16   court and they have not been convicted of a crime, and

17   they chose to accept a discussion with community members

18   and a board and then act as they were asked, which was

19   to do some community service for a worthy organization.

20   I don't know how that can be a bad thing,

21   but it seems to me in sentencing here today to sentence

22   to something less than that would not be just, and I'm

23   not going to do that, but I'm certainly not going to

24   impose another jail sentence.

25   And so with all of that said, the most

```
 1    appropriate sentence I can come up with is as follows.
 2    It's a zero to two-day sentence.  It's suspended and
 3    administrative probation.  Administrative probation
 4    means there's no supervision whatsoever.
 5               The only conditions are that you attend
 6    the reparative board.  I'm sorry you find that word
 7    offensive.  It's not I don't think.  It is not designed
 8    or set out for some form of humiliation.  It is actually
 9    an opportunity for you to sit down and discuss what
10    you'd like with some other people.
11               You can choose to accept what they
12    suggest you should do to make amends if they do or not.
13    That will be your decision, of course, but I'd encourage
14    you at least to go through with it and hear what they
15    have to say.  It seems to me you'd like to speak about
16    this in any event, and talking to some people directly
17    about it makes perfect sense to me.  I hope it does to
18    you.  They'll tell you what they think should be done.
19    You can accept it or not at that point.
20               So it will be a reparative board
21    sentence.  That is, zero to two days suspended,
22    administrative probation, so you're entitled to
23    certainly that day.  It counts as a day.  And the only
24    condition is that you attend and complete the reparative
25    board program.  Again it will be your choice whether to
```

1 do that or not. There are sanctions if you don't, but

2 that's up to you. I'd encourage you at least to sit

3 down with those people and talk to them. They deserve

4 that as much as you do.

5   Concerning the stay, Mr. Saltonstall, I

6 just need a couple minutes. I want to read the case.

7 It is unfortunate it wasn't presented during the trial,

8 but we will take a look at it shortly, and if I agree

9 with you that at least there's a reasonable chance of

10 success, then certainly you're entitled to a stay. If

11 not, I think we'll just move right along. So if you

12 just give me a couple minutes (inaudible).

13   MR. SALTONSTALL: Thank you, Judge.

14   THE COURT: Thank you all.

15 (Thereupon, the proceedings were concluded.)

CERTIFICATE

    I, Donna Gould, do certify that the foregoing

pages, numbered 2 through 51, inclusive, are a true and

accurate transcription, to the best of my ability, of

the proceedings held on October 7, 2004, in the matter

of State v. Rose Marie Jackowski held in the Bennington

District Court.

                              Donna Gould

                              Transcriber